THE PLACE WHERE HELL BUBBLED UP

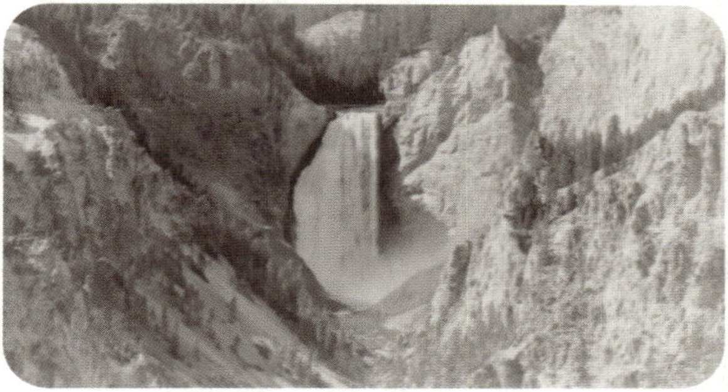

A HISTORY OF THE FIRST NATIONAL PARK

BY DAVID A. CLARY

To Nancy & Warren
Thank you for your friendship
Bob & Mary Rose

WY Bishop Bob Jones

HOMESTEAD PUBLISHING
Moose, Wyoming

1994

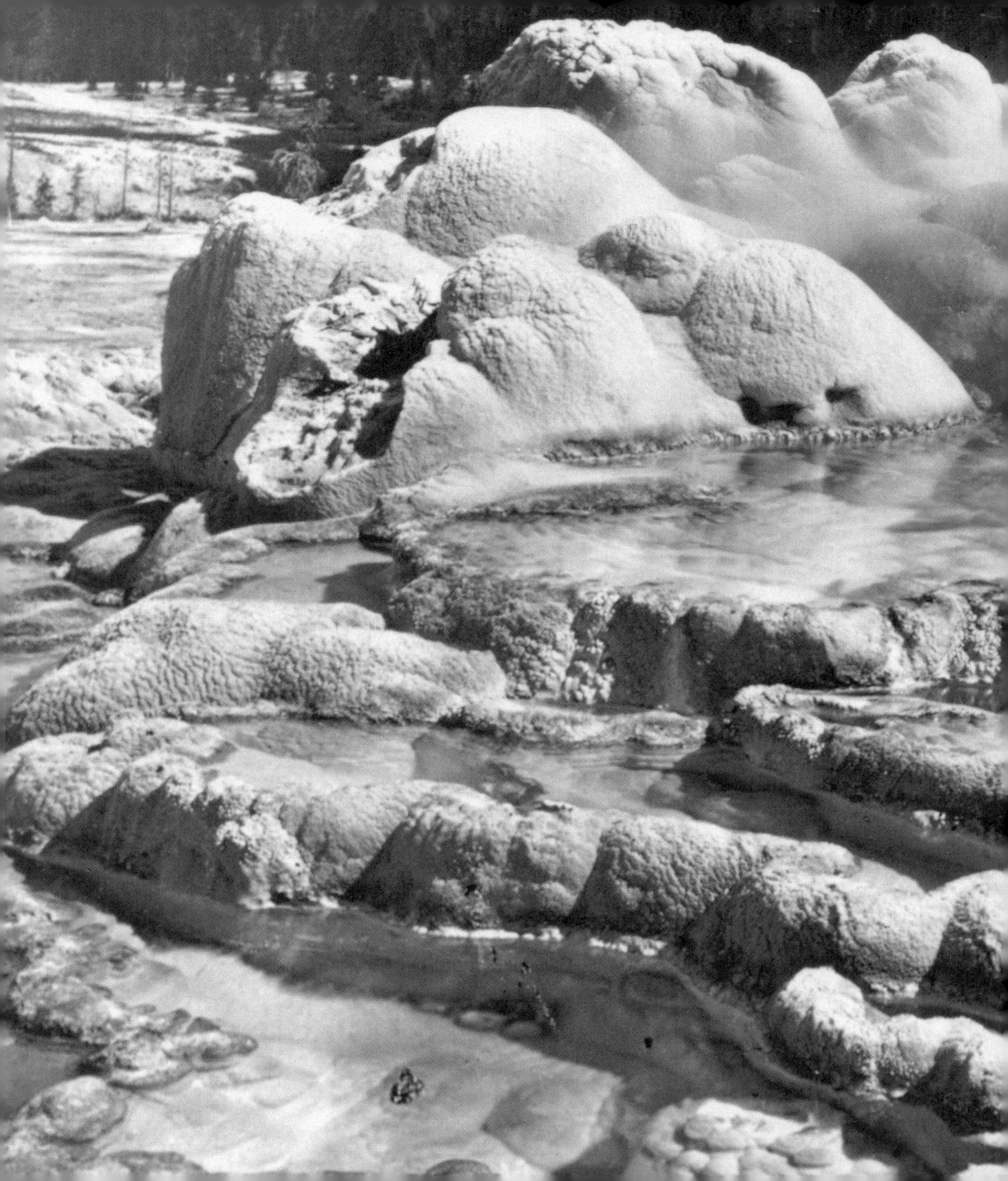

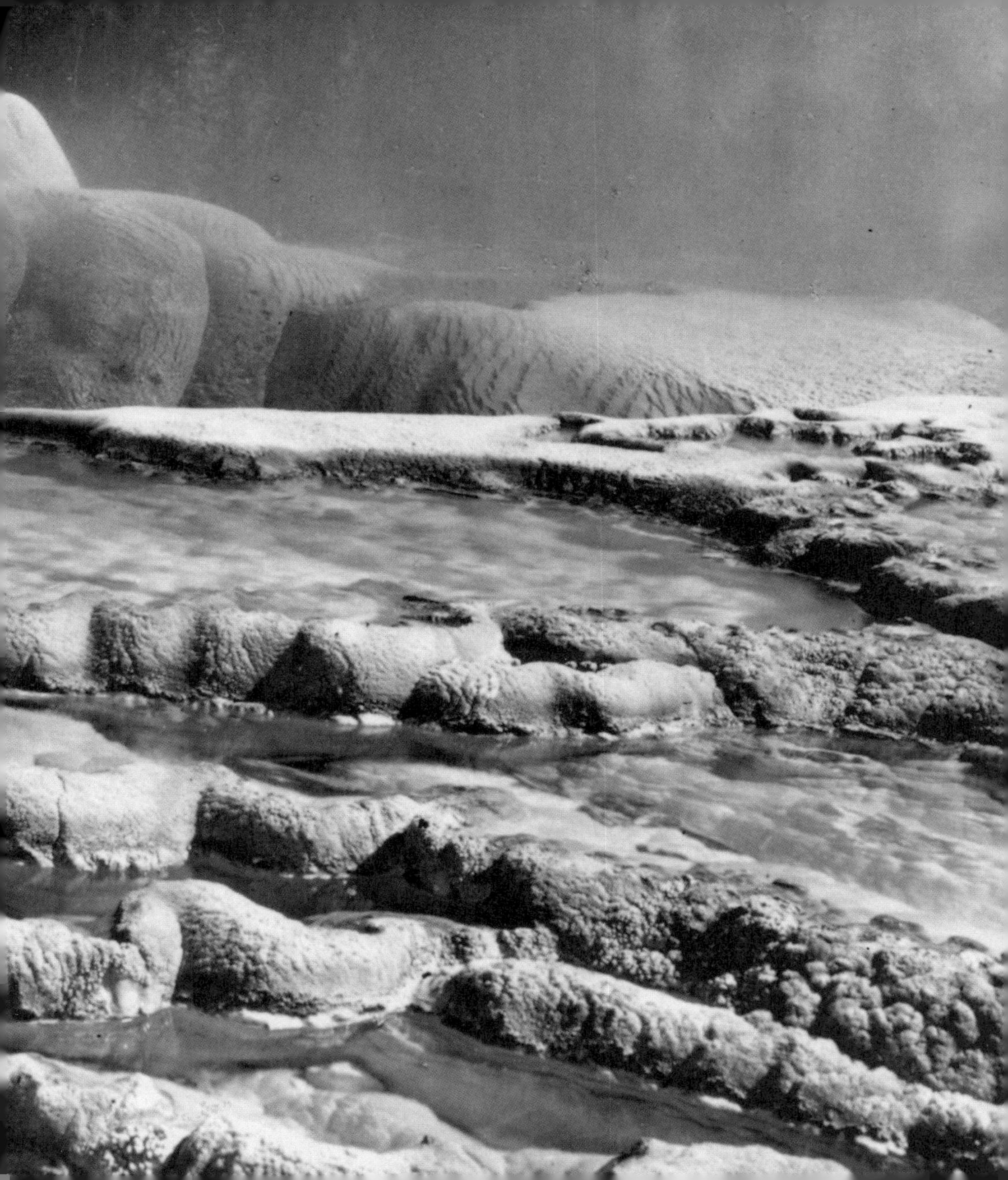

ISBN 0-943972-19-1
Library of Congress Catalog Card Number 93-77119
Homestead Publishing 1993
Printed in U.S.A. on acid free, recycled paper

Published by
HOMESTEAD PUBLISHING
Box 193
Moose, Wyoming 83012

PHOTOGRAPHIC CREDITS
Cover photo: Hayden Valley.
Back cover: Hot Spring Cone, (Fishing Cone) Yellowstone Lake, c. 1883.
Cover map: From F.V. Hayden's 1872 Geological Survey of the Territories.
Back cover quote: From F. Dumont Smith's 1909, Book of a Hundred Bears.
Title page: Lower Falls of the Grand Canyon of the Yellowstone.
*Preface Page (Previous page): The Upper Geyser Basin with the cone of Old Faithful
in the foreground, taken by the pioneer photographer William Henry Jackson in 1872
on his second trip into the region of the Yellowstone with the Hayden Expedition.*

THE IDEA OF YELLOWSTONE

One morning in May 1834, in what is now the northwest corner of Wyoming three men waited anxiously for the end of a night of strange noises and curious smells. Warren Ferris, a clerk for the American Fur Company, had ventured into the upper Yellowstone country with two Indian companions to find out for himself the truth about the wild tales trappers told about the region. It was a place, they said, of hot springs, water volcanoes, noxious gases, and terrifying vibrations. The water volcanoes especially interested him, and now, as dawn broke over the Upper Geyser Basin, Ferris looked out on an unforgettable scene:

Clouds of vapor seemed like a dense fog to overhang the spring, from which frequent reports or explosions of different loudness, constantly assailed our ears. I immediately proceeded to inspect them, and might have exclaimed with the Queen of Sheba, when their full reality of dimensions and novelty burst upon my view, "The half was not told me." From the surface of a rocky plain or table, burst forth columns of water, of various dimensions, projected high in the air, accompanied by loud explosions, and sulphurous vapors. . . . The largest of these wonderful fountains, projects a column of boiling water several feet in diameter, to the height of more than one hundred and fifty feet accompanied with a tremendous noise. . . . I ventured near enough to put my hand into the water of its basin, but withdrew it instantly, for the heat of the water in this immense cauldron, was altogether too great for comfort, and the agitation of the water... and the hollow unearthly rumbling under the rock on which I stood, so ill accorded with my notions of personal safety, that I retreated back precipitately to a respectful distance.

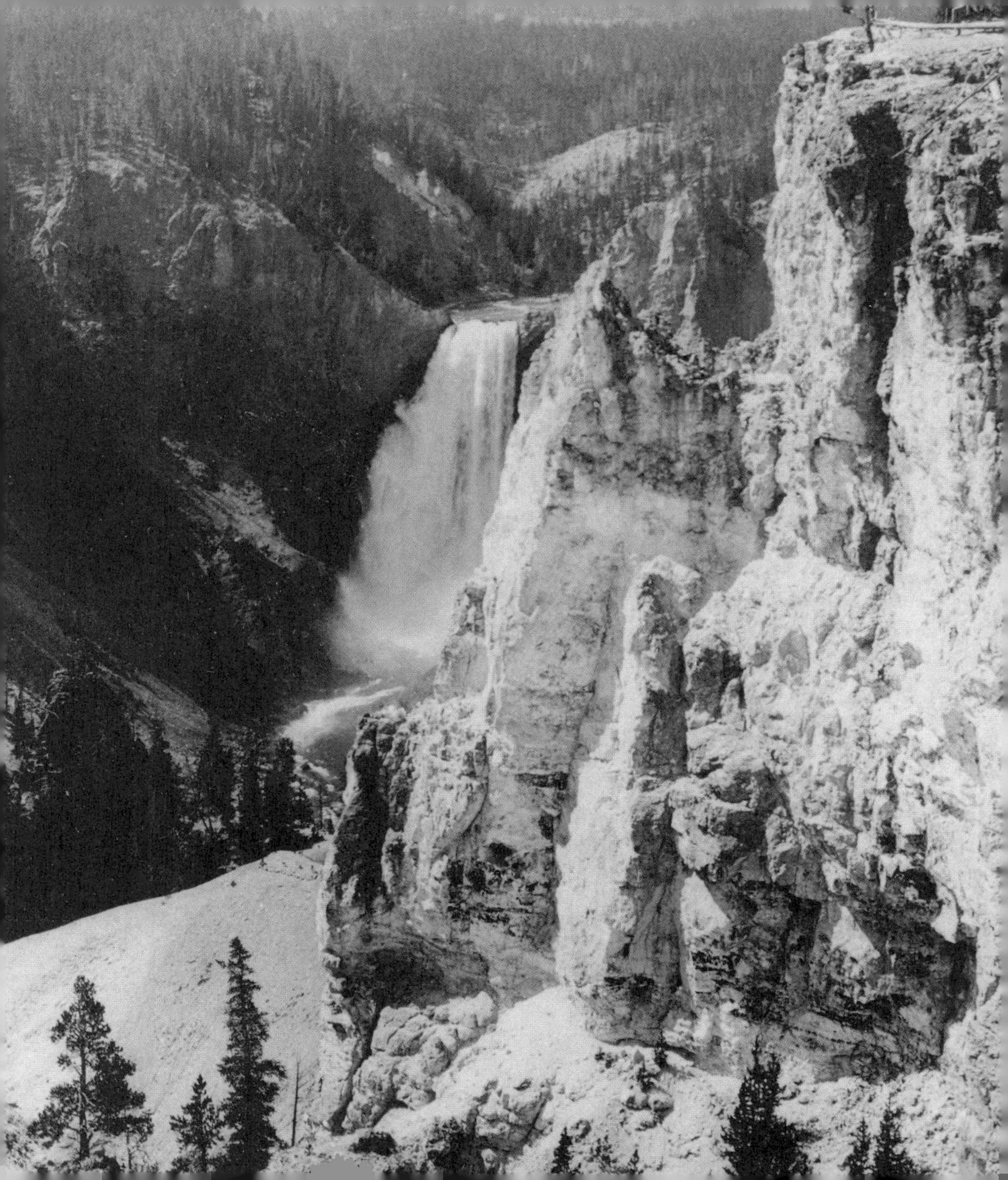

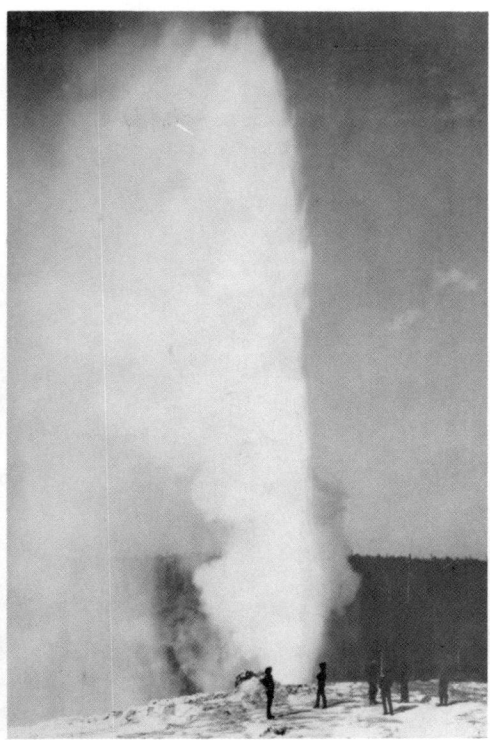

Members of the Hayden party, which explored the Yellowstone region in 1871, 1872 and 1878, observe the eruption of Old Faithul. At left is Jackson's record of Tower Creek above the brink of the falls.

Ferdinand V. Hayden, leader of the 1871 expedition, remarked that "no language can do justice to the wonderful grandeur and beauty of the cañon below the Lower Falls (left); the very nearly vertical walls, slightly sloping down to the water's edge on either side, so that from the summit the river appears like a thread of silver foaming over its rocky bottom; the variegated colors of the sides, yellow, red, brown, white, all intermixed and shading into each other; the Gothic columns of every form standing out from the sides of the walls with greater variety and more striking colors than ever adorned a work of human art."

/7

On the 28th of July, 1871, the Hayden party arrived at Yellowstone Lake. "The entire party were filled with enthusiam," wrote Hayden in his journal. The party set up camp on the quiet waters of Mary Bay and proclaimed "one of the most beautiful scenes I have ever beheld. . . The great object of all our labors had been reached, and we were amply paid for all our toils."

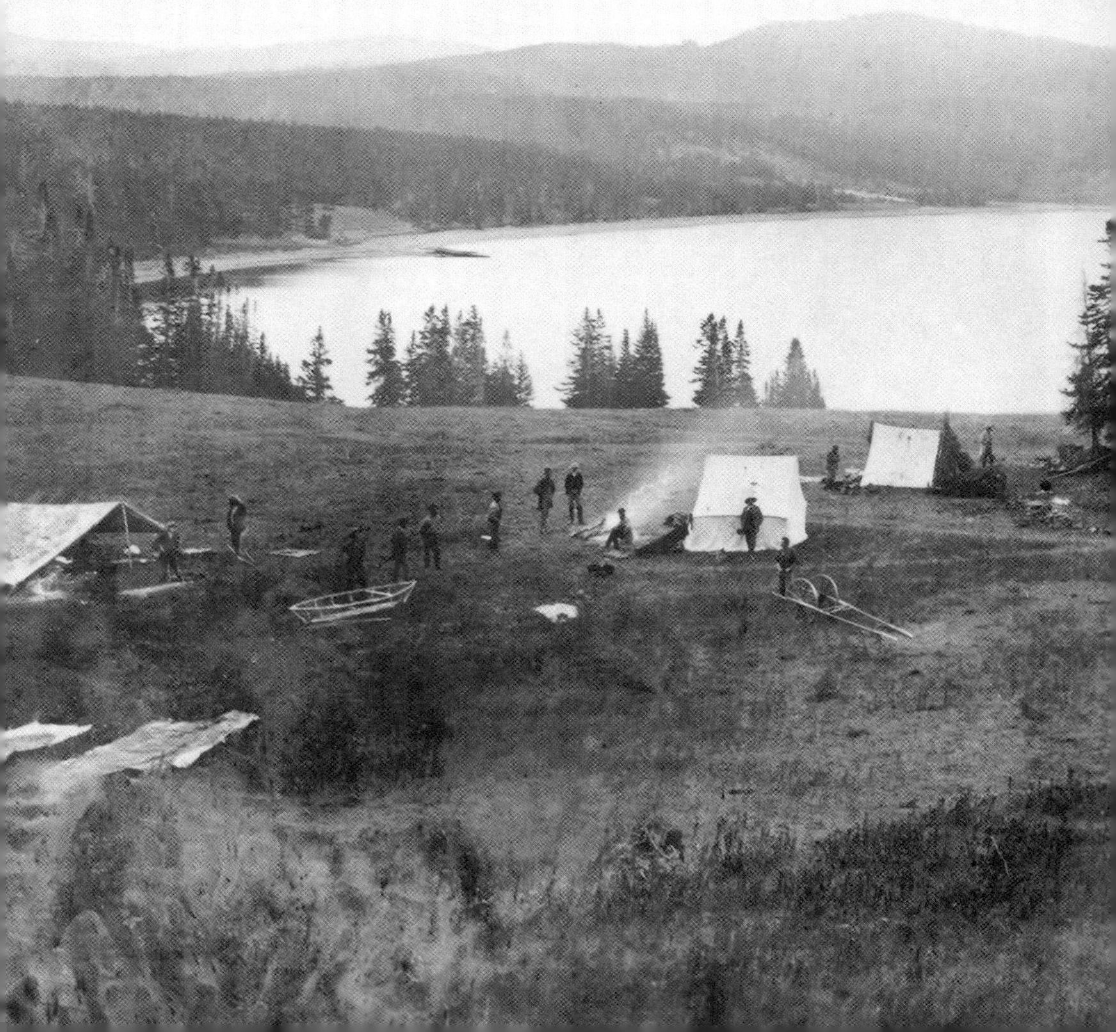

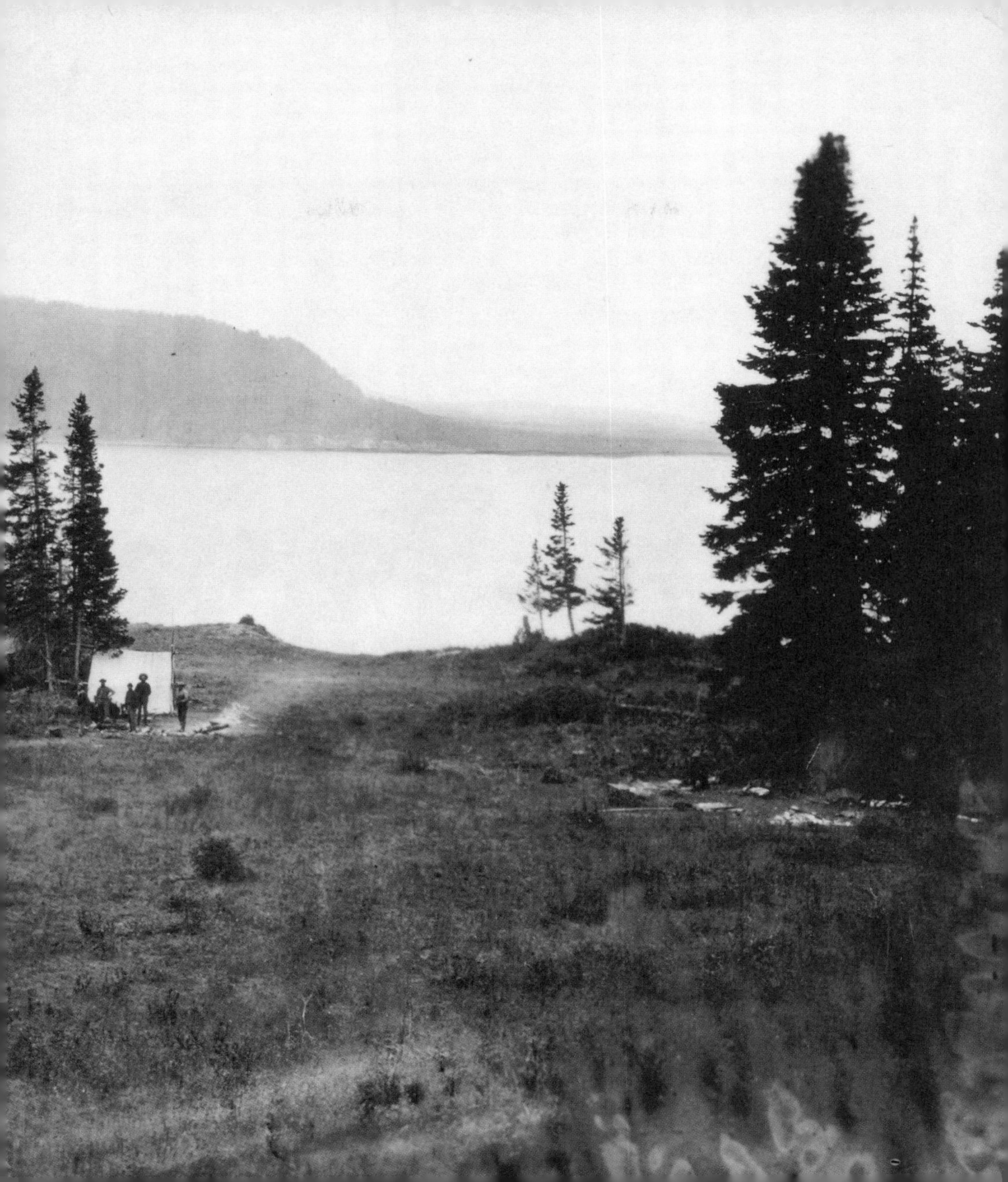

William H. Jackson considered Castle Geyser, in the Upper Geyser Basin, one of the most spectacular thermal features in Yellowstone. He stated, "Here we see the peculiar crystallization of the silica in large globular masses, like spongiform corals, and running off into the usual exquisite beadwork to the laminated base. The entire mound is about 40 feet in height. In the center of the view, and the most striking object in it, is the beautiful hot spring, [Crested Pool] with elegantly carved border and water of the clearest turquoise blue. The water is of almost unnatural clearness, and the varying depth gives a most beautiful gradation of color."

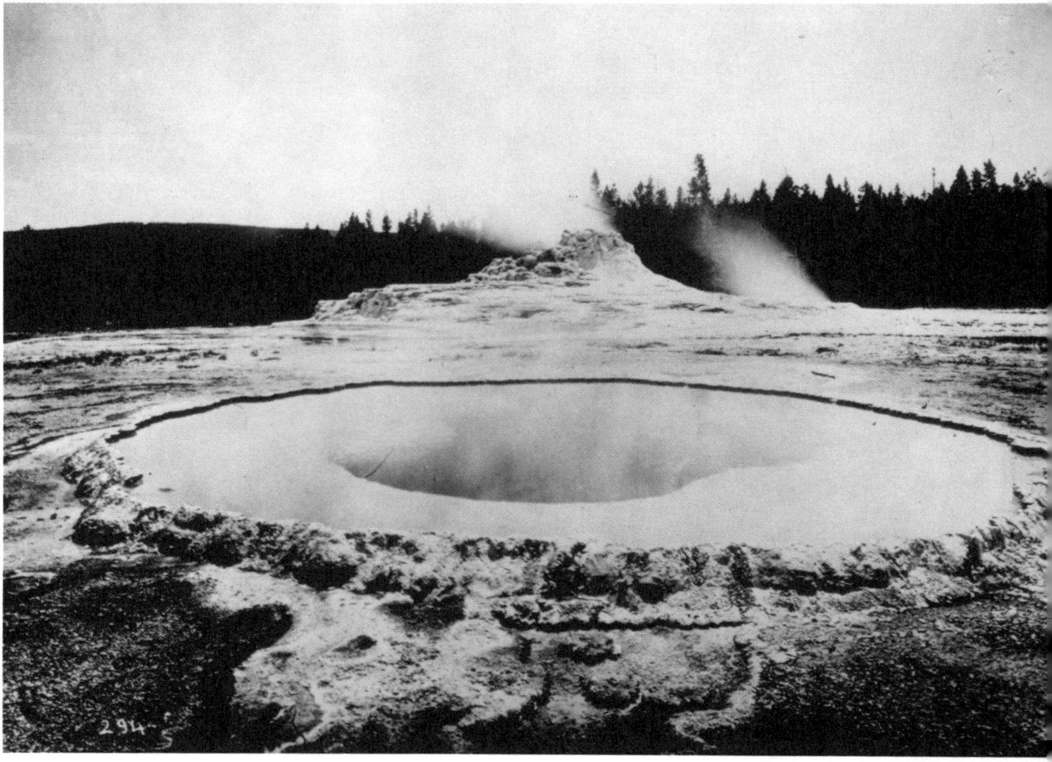
294

Ferris later recalled that his companions thought it unwise to trifle with the supernatural:

> *The Indians who were with me, were quite appalled, and could not by any means be induced to approach them. They seemed astonished at my presumption in advancing up to the large one, and when I safely returned, congratulated me on my "narrow escape". . . . One of them remarked that hell, of which he had heard from the whites, must be in that vicinity.*

Ferris and his friends quickly concluded their excursion and went back to earning a living in the fur trade. They had not been the first visitors to this land of geysers. But they were the first who came as "tourists," having no purpose other than to see the country.

It was the awesome evidence of this land's great volcanic past that drew Ferris and his comrades, and others after them, into an uncharted wilderness. For whatever the other attractions of this region—and there are many—man has reacted most to this spectacle of a great dialectic of nature, this apparent duel between the hot earth and the waters that continually attempt to invade it.

Seething mud pots, hot pools of delicate beauty, hissing vents, periodic earthquakes, and sudden frightening geysers are foreign to our ordinary experience. But in this region a wonderful variety of such features, seeming to speak of powers beyond human comprehension, confronts visitors at every turn. So it is easy to understand why many observers have speculated, along with the companions of Warren Ferris, that this may indeed be near the dark region of the white man's religion.

Yet this Biblical metaphor, which came so naturally to men of the 19th century, fails to evoke the full sense of Yellowstone. Lt. Gustavus C. Doane, who explored the country of the celebrated 1870 expedition, thought that "No figure of imagination, no description of enchantment, can equal in imagery the vista of these great mountains." There is the stately lodgepole forest, the ranging wildlife, the fantastic geyser, and the great lake, and there is the mighty torrent of the Yellowstone River, the spectacular waterfalls, and the rugged, many-hued chasm from which the river and ultimately the region took its name. And beyond all this, there is Yellowstone the symbol. The notion that a wilderness should be set aside and perpetuated for the benefit of all the people has flowered beyond the wildest dreams of those who conceived it.

This is the story, in broadest outline, of the people who have visited this remarkable country, of their influence upon it, and of Yellowstone's influence upon them. It begins long ago, as all such stories must on the American continent, with the Native American.

THE MARK OF EARLY MAN

For more than 10,000 years people have trod the Yellowstone wilderness. In the beginning human visits were rare and brief. Those who approached the vicinity of Yellowstone were already many generations and thousands of miles removed from their ancestral Asian origins, and most of them in the early days came to the region to hunt rather than to live.

The first men arrived during the decline of the last ice age. Their small and highly mobile population possessed a limited material culture and left little physical evidence of their presence—mainly distinctive stone tools and projectile points now classified under such terms as "Folsom" and "Clovis." They traveled along rivers and down major valleys in pursuit of such denizens of the ice age as the mammoth, the ancestral horse, and the giant bison, as well as the familiar animals of today. They supplemented game with berries, seeds, and roots. Though they were few in number, their weapons and tools made them comparatively efficient, and their hunting combined with the warming of the climate, may have contributed to the disappearance of many primeval mammals. When the last glacial stage ended about 8,500 years ago, many animals that were adapted to colder, wetter conditions became extinct. This environmental change also altered the habits of man.

As the climate in the Yellowstone region warmed up, the surrounding plains grew extremely hot and dry but mountainous areas remained well watered. The population in the region increased steadily as a new lifeway—hunting for small game and foraging for plants—replaced the endless wandering of the original hunters. Hunting could be done more efficiently after the small bands acquired the bow and arrow, and so large game became more prominent in the diet of man in Yellowstone.

By about 1600 Yellowstone was occupied by semi-nomadic populations that left many stone tools and projectile points, domestic utensils, and campsites. When the horse arrived in the high country of the West in the late 17th century, it upset old Indian patterns of living, and in some places produced entirely new cultures. The Indians could now follow the bison herds and other gregarious game of the plains. Mountain areas, more difficult to travel over by horseback, rapidly lost much of their population. When the first frontiersmen came to Yellowstone in the early 19th century, few people were living there. Only occasional hunting parties of Crows, Blackfeet, and Bannocks crossed its vastness, while small bands of Shoshones lived in its mountains.

The Crows occupied the country generally east of the present park and the Blackfeet that to the north. The Shoshonean Bannocks and probably other tribes of the plateaus to the northwest traversed the area annually to hunt on the plains to the east. But other Shoshonean groups were probably more influenced by the horse. They had been pushing northward along the eastern edge of the Great Basin (west and south of the park), and the acquisition of horses both intensified this movement and scattered them in diverse bands. About 1700 the Comanches separated themselves from the rest of the Western Shoshones and moved southeastward into the plains. Most of the Shoshones hunted in the open areas west and south of Yellowstone. But some, either through the conservatism of their culture of the lack of opportunity, did not acquire horses. They continued to hunt and forage on foot in the mountains of Yellowstone, where there was little competition. A band of these people occupied the highlands until 1871, when they rejoined their kinsmen on the Wind River Reservation in west-central Wyoming. Because of the importance of mountain sheep in their diet, they had become known as "Sheepeaters." Their occupation left no more mark on the land than did the occasional visits of Crows, Blackfeet, or other Shoshones. After they left and the tribes from the outside ceased to hunt in Yellowstone, only the scattered ruins of the hearth sites and brush and pole lodges, called wickiups, that had once been their simple homes remained.

Yellowstone was the crossroads for nomadic Indian tribes who traversed the high mountain plateau during the summers to hunt for game, fish the rivers and collect berries and herbs. The Crows occupied the country to the east of the present park and their rivals, the Blackfeet, the country to the north. The Shoshone Indians (above—encamped at South Pass on the southern foothills of the Wind River Mountains, 1870) came from the south and they all met on neutral ground—Yellowstone. The only people who inhabited Yellowstone year-round were a small band of sheepeaters, who were named because of the importance of bighorn sheep in their diet. They were mountain dwellers related to the Bannock and Shoshone Indians.

/13

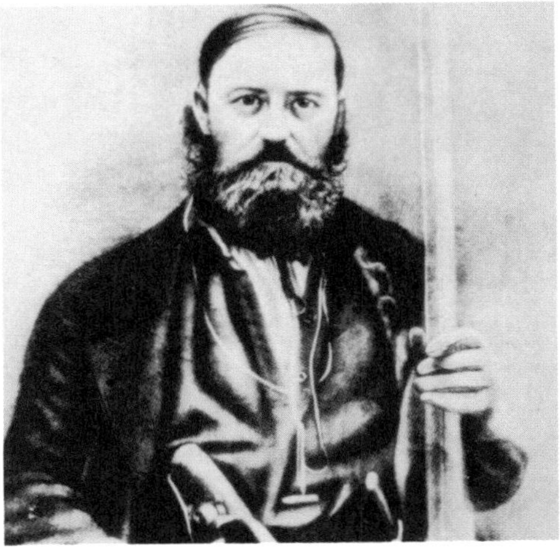

Joseph L. Meek, kin to President Polk, was a legendary trapper during the early 1800s.

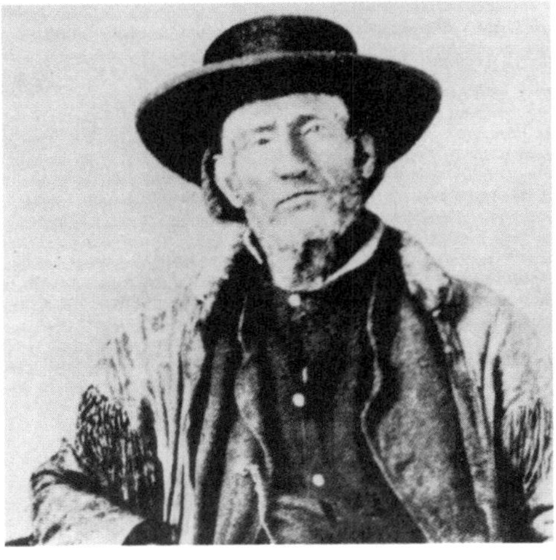

Jim Bridger's tall tales popularized the wonders of Yellowstone but made them unbelievable.

During the late 18th century those wandering heralds of civilization, the fur trappers, filtered into the upper Missouri country in search of a broad-tailed promise of fortune—the beaver. The early trappers and traders were mostly French Canadian, and the great tributary of the Missouri, the Yellowstone, first became known to white men by its French label, "Roche Jaune." None of the earliest trappers, however, seem to have observed the thermal activity in the area that would some day become a national park, although they probably learned of some of its wonders from their Indian acquaintances.

The Lewis and Clark Expedition passed just north of Yellowstone in 1806. Though Indians told them of the great lake, they remained unaware of the areas's hot springs and geysers. While Lewis and Clark were exploring the Northwest, a trader appeared in St. Louis with an Indian map drawn on a buffalo hide. This rude sketch showed the region of the upper Yellowstone and indicated the presence of what appeared to be "a volcano. . . on Yellow Stone River." After his return to St. Louis, Clark interviewed an Indian who had been to the area and reported: "There is a frequently heard a loud noise like Thunder, which makes the earth Tremble, they state that they seldom go there because their children cannot sleep—and Conceive it possessed of spirits, who were averse that men Should be near them." But civilized men were not yet wholly ready to believe "a savage delineation," preferring to withhold judgment until one of their own kind reported his observations.

In 1807 Manuel Lisa's Missouri Fur Trading Company constructed Fort Raymond at the confluence of the Bighorn and Yellowstone Rivers as a center for trading with the Indians. To attract clients, Lisa sent John Colter on a harrowing 500-mile journey through untracked Indian country. A veteran of the Lewis and Clark Expedition, Colter was a man born "for hardy indurance of fatigue, privation and perils." Part of his route in 1807-8 is open to conjecture, but he is known to have skirted the northwest shore of Yellowstone Lake and crossed the Yellowstone River near Tower Falls, where he noted the presence of "Hot Spring Brimstone." Although a thermal area near present-day Cody, Wyoming, later became famous among trappers as "Colter's Hell," Colter is more celebrated as the first white man know to have entered Yellowstone. The privations of a trapper's life and a narrow escape from the Blackfeet in 1808 prompted him to leave the mountains forever in 1810. But he was the pioneer, and for three decades a procession of beaver hunters followed in his footsteps.

Though most of the trappers who entered Yellowstone were Americans working for various companies or as free traders, some Canadians also visited the region in the early days. At least one party of Hudson's Bay Company men left a cache of beaver traps within the park. By 1824 Yellowstone seems to have been fairly well known to most trappers, judging by the casual note of one in his journal: "Saturday 24th—we crossed beyond the Boiling Fountains. The snow is knee deep." In 1827 a Philadelphia newspaper printed a letter from a trapper who described his experiences hunting furs and fighting Blackfeet in Yellowstone. This letter was the first published description of the region:

on the south borders of this lake is a number of hot and boiling springs some of water and others of most beautiful fine clay and resembles that of a mush pot and throws its particles to the immense height of from twenty to thirty feet in height. The clay is white and pink and water appear fathomless as it appears to be entirely hollow underneath. There is also a number of places where the pure sulphor is sent forth in abundance one of our men visited one of these whilst taking his recreation at an instan [sic] made his escape when an explosion took place resembling that of thunder. During our stay in that quarter I heard it every day. . . .

After 1826, American trappers apparently hunted within the future park every year. Joe Meek, one of the best known of the early beaver men, expressed the surprise of some of these early visitors: "behold! the

/15

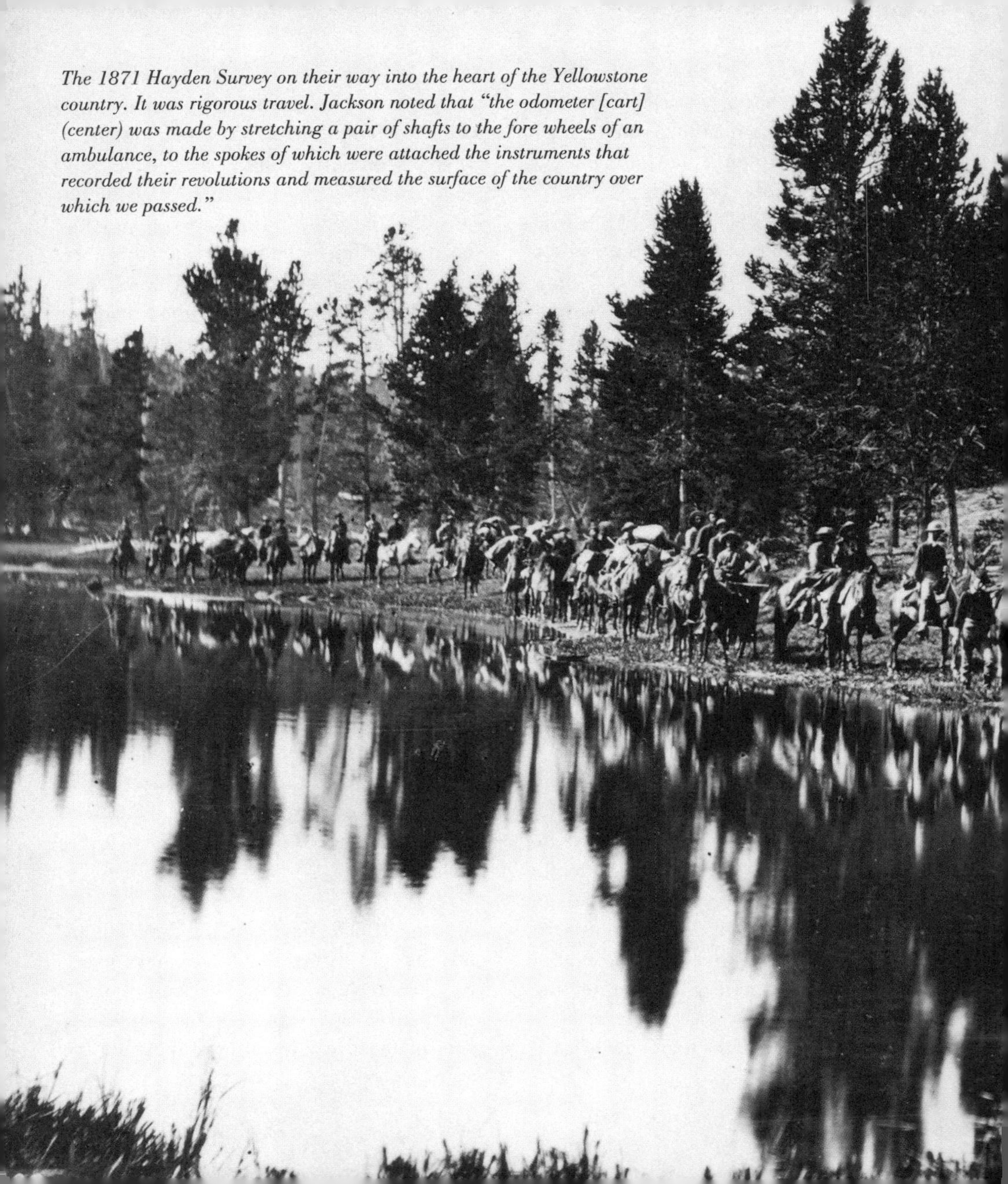

The 1871 Hayden Survey on their way into the heart of the Yellowstone country. It was rigorous travel. Jackson noted that "the odometer [cart] (center) was made by stretching a pair of shafts to the fore wheels of an ambulance, to the spokes of which were attached the instruments that recorded their revolutions and measured the surface of the country over which we passed."

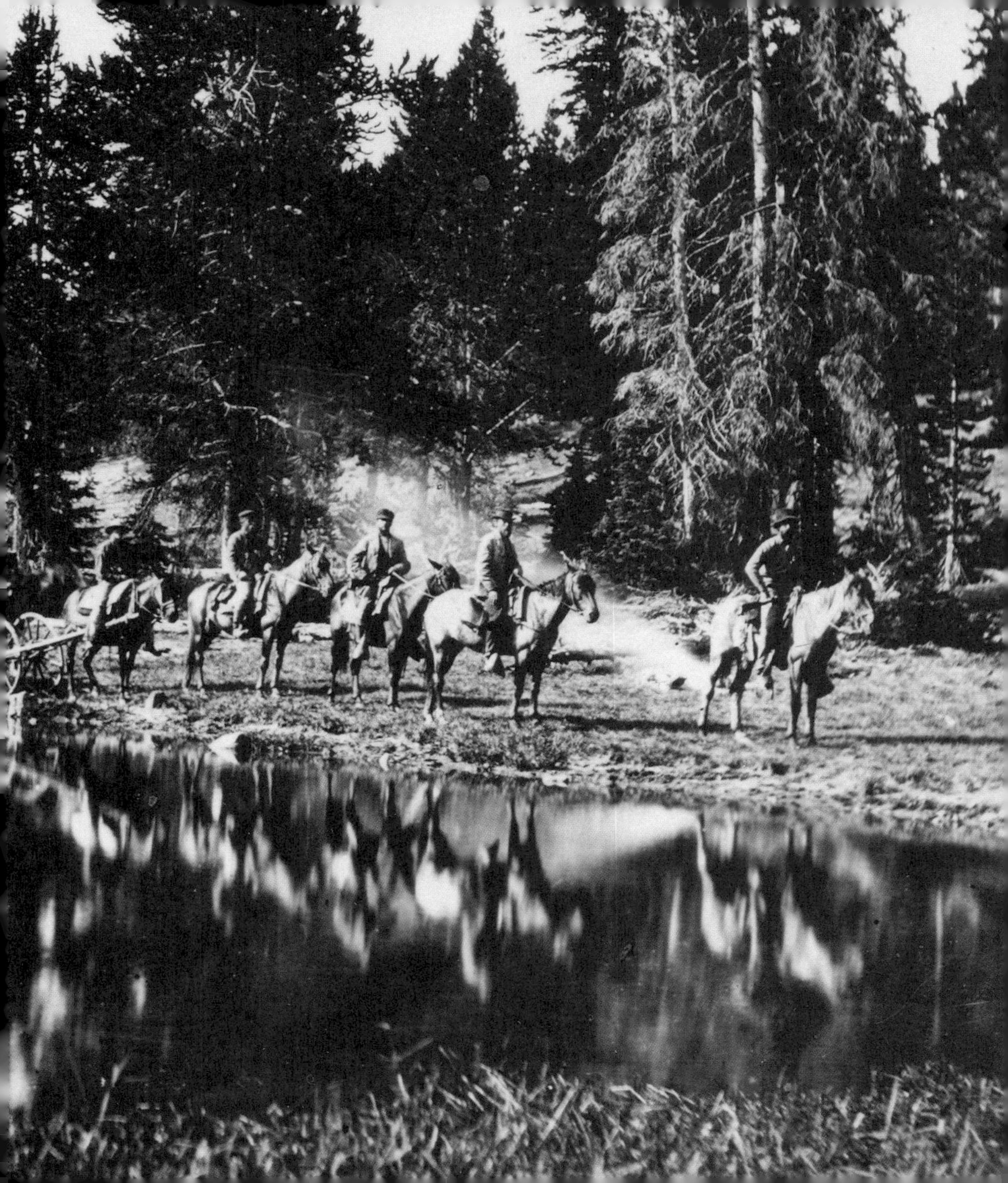

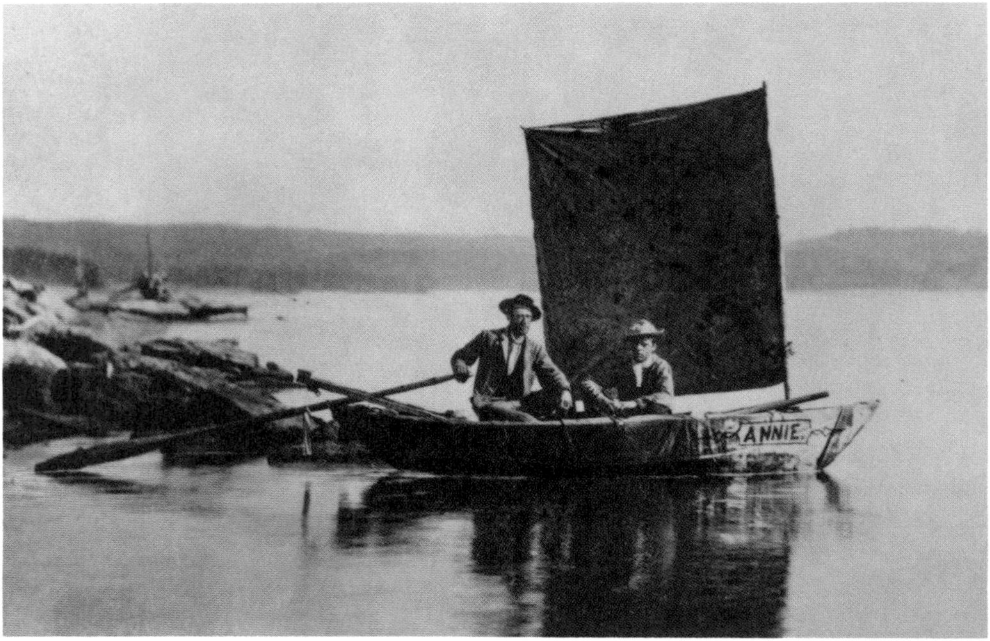
ANNIE

"Annie," the first boat on Yellowstone Lake, was built and launched during the 1871 expedition. The small boat frame, "12 feet long and 3½ feet wide. . . covered with stout ducking, well tarred" was carried by the party, erected, and christened the "Anna. . . in compliment to Miss Anna L. Dawes, the amiable daughter of Hon. H. L. Dawes—the distinguished statesman whose generous sympathy and aid had contributed so much toward securing the appropriation which enabled them to explore this marvelous region."

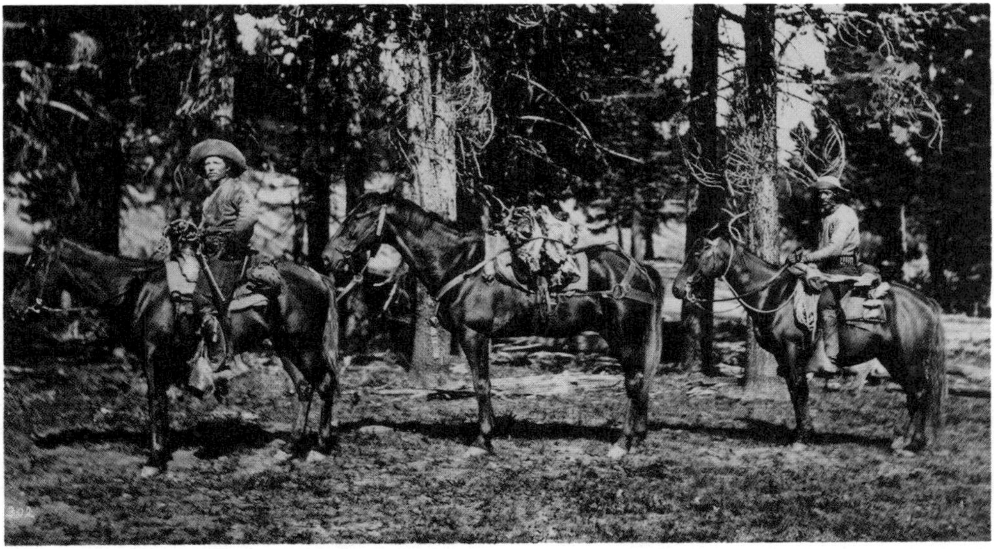

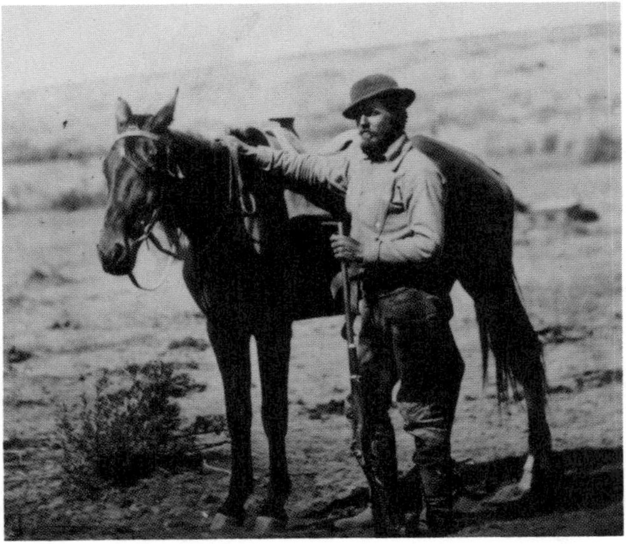

Hunters, José and Joe Clark, with the 1872 Hayden expedition, return from a successful hunt, with their pack animal laden with elk meat.

Jackson's self-portrait. He was the official photographer for the 1871, 1872 and 1878 expeditions into Yellowstone.

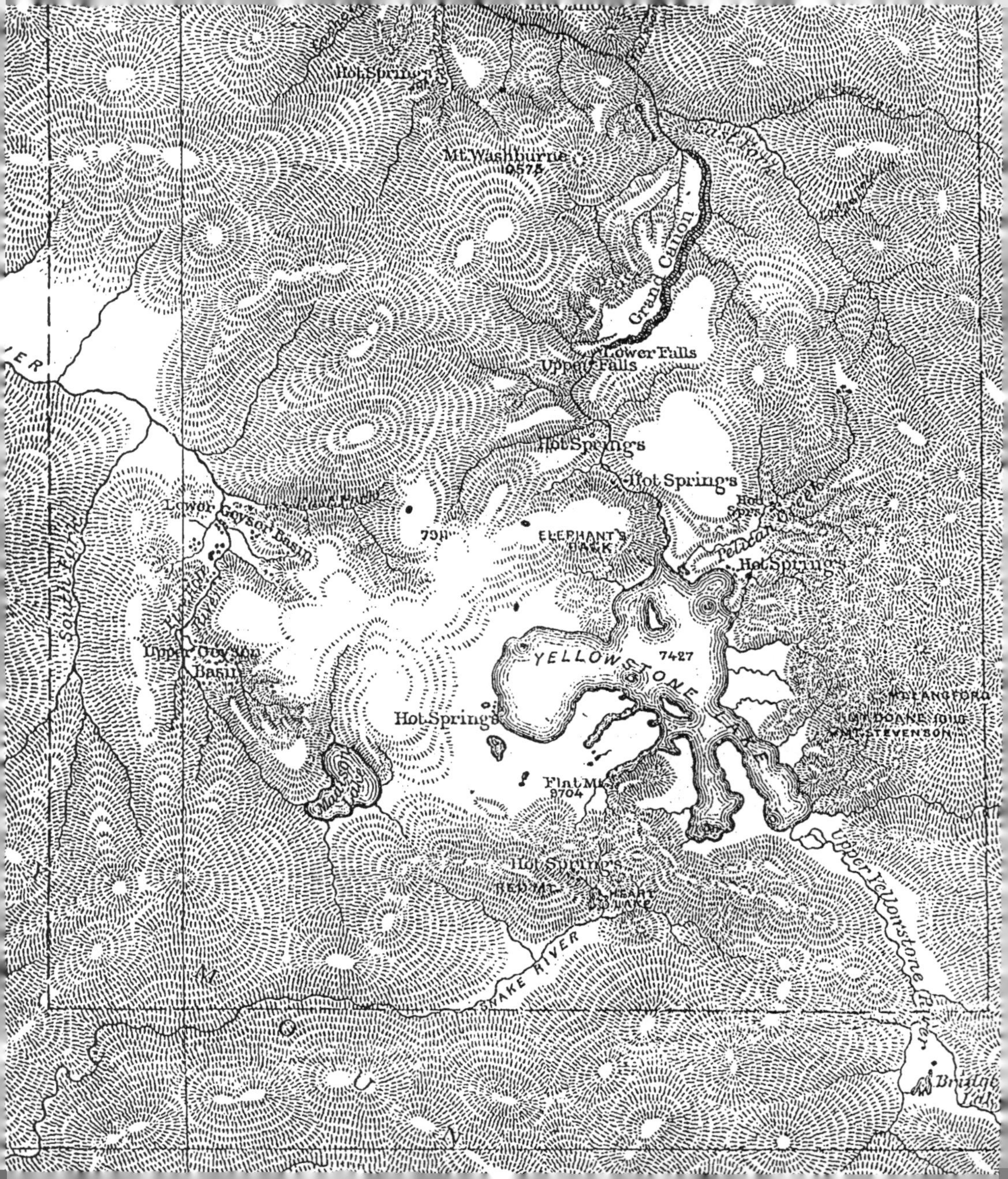
Hot Springs
Mt. Washburne
Grand Cañon
East Fork
Lower Falls
Upper Falls
Hot Springs
Hot Springs
Lower Geyser Basin
Upper Geyser Basin
ELEPHANT'S BACK
Pelican
Hot Springs
YELLOWSTONE LAKE
7427
Hot Springs
MT. DOANE
MT. STEVENSON
Flat Mt.
9704
Hot Springs
RED MT.
HEART LAKE
SNAKE RIVER
Upper Yellowstone River

Ferdinand V. Hayden, at left, who led the 1871, 1872 and 1878 explorations of Yellowstone, talks with his assistant Walter Paris.

Hayden's published map of the 1871 expedition of the Yellowstone region. Note the region south of Yellowstone, now known as Grand Teton, was unexplored until the following year.

/21

whole country beyond was smoking with the vapor from boiling springs, and burning with gasses." Such reaction, however, gradually gave way to casual acceptance of the thermal activity.

Trappers had little for entertainment but talk; as a class they were the finest of storytellers. Verbal embellishment became a fine art as they related their experiences fighting Indians or visiting strange country. Perhaps the greatest of the yarn spinners was Jim Bridger. Though it is doubtful he told them all, tradition links his name with many of Yellowstone's tall tales.

In 1856 a Kansas City newspaper editor rejected as patent lies Bridger's lucid description of the Yellowstone wonders. Perhaps this sort of refusal to believe the truth about "the place where Hell bubbled up," as Bridger called Yellowstone, led him and other trappers to embellish their accounts with false detail. They related their visits to the petrified forest, carpeted with petrified grass, populated with petrified animals and containing even birds petrified in flight. They told of the shrinking qualities of Alum Creek, the banks of which were frequented by miniature animals. Fish caught in the cold water at the bottom of a curious spring were cooked passing through the hot water on top. Elk hunters bumped into a glass mountain. Such stories gave the features of Yellowstone the reputation of fantasies concocted by trapper. But the spread of this lore caused a few to wonder whether some fact might not lie behind the fancy.

By about 1840 the extirpation of the beaver and the popularity of the silk hat had combined to end the day of the trapper. For almost 20 years, Yellowstone, only rarely visited by white men, was left to the Indians. By the time of the Civil War, however, the relentless westward push of civilization and the burning memory of California gold drew to Yellowstone another herald of the frontier—the prospector. A rich strike was made in Montana in 1862, and the resultant stampede brought a horde of men to that territory. Despite often fatal discouragements from Indians, their lust for gold was such that they filtered into nearly every part of Yellowstone, but found not a sparkle of the magic metal. One enterprising gold seeker, a civil engineer and soldier of fortune named Walter W. deLacy, published in 1865 the first reasonably accurate map of the Yellowstone region. By the time the gold rush had died out in the late 1860s, the future national park had been thoroughly examined by prospectors. Although they were even greater liars than the mountain men, their tales of the wondrous land they had seen planted a seed of curiosity in Montana that was to impel others to take a careful look for themselves.

THE COUNTRY DISCOVERED

Although Yellowstone had been thoroughly tracked by trappers and miners, in the view of the Nation at large it was really "discovered" when penetrated by formal expeditions originating in the settlements of an expanding America.

The first organized attempt to explore Yellowstone came in 1860. Capt. William F. Raynolds, a discerning Army engineer guided by Jim Bridger, led a military expedition that accomplished much but failed to penetrate the future park because of faulty scheduling and early snow. The Civil War preoccupied the Government during the next few years. During the late 1860s, however, stories of the area's wonders so excited many of Montana's leading citizens and officials that several explorations were planned. But none actually got underway.

Indian trouble and lack of a military escort caused the abandonment of the last such expedition in the summer of 1869. Determined that they would not be deprived of a look at the wondrous region, three members of that would-be venture—David E. Folsom, Charles W. Cook, and William Peterson—decided to make the trek anyway. Folsom and Cook brought with them a sensitivity to nature endowed by a Quaker upbringing, while Peterson displayed the hardy spirit that came from years as a seafarer. All three, futhermore, had become

Dr. Ferdinand Vandiveer Hayden, physician, surgeon, geologist, paleontologist, mineralogist, and director of the U.S. Geological Surveys, led the famous 1871 Hayden expedition into Yellowstone. During that summer 35 men—20 scientists and artists and 15 soldiers—made a complete reconnaissance of the remote region, charting its features, collecting specimens, photographing and sketching its wonders. They documented the existence of Yellowstone to the world and convinced Congress of its importance. The Park Bill was signed the following spring by President Ulysses S. Grant on March 1, 1872.

/23

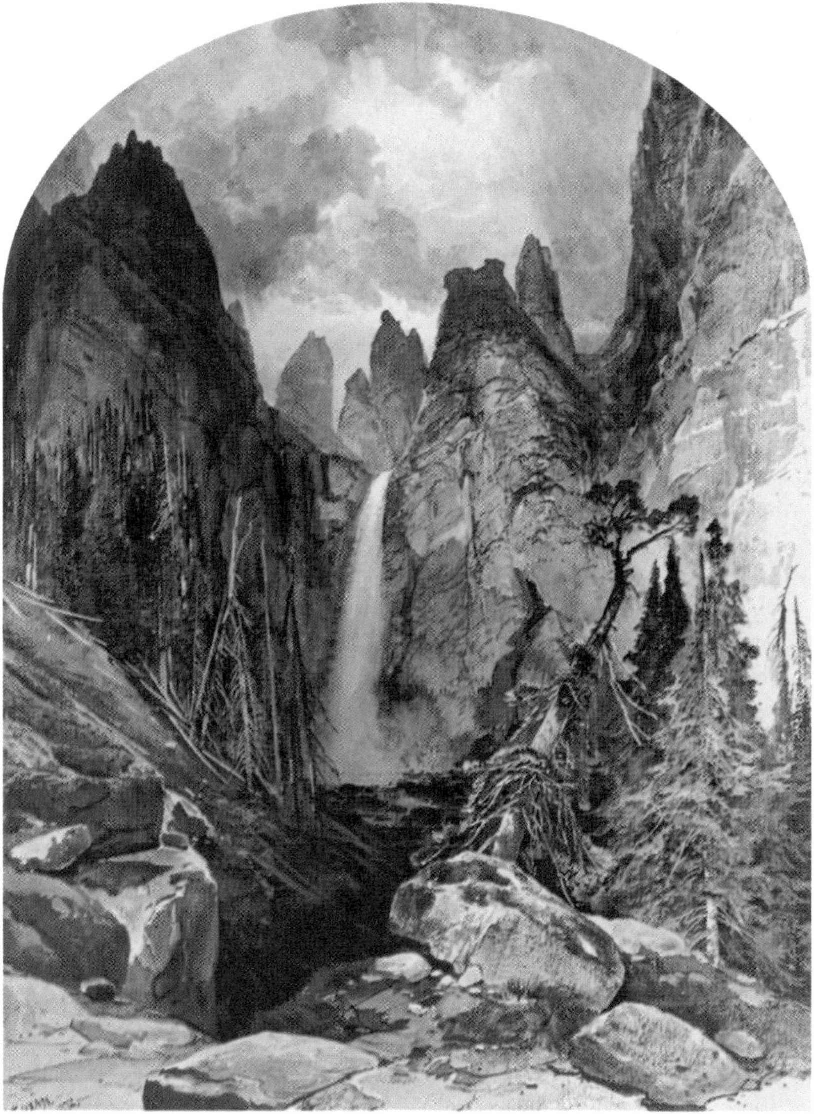

The paintings of artist Thomas Moran—watercolor of Tower Falls (left)—and the photographs of William Henry Jackson were instrumental in helping pass the National Park Act, creating Yellowstone National Park. Jackson's photograph depicting Moran (above) climbing on Mammoth Hot Springs was one of the first photographs taken in Yellowstone.

experienced frontiersmen while prospecting for Montana gold. They acquired a store of provisions, armed themselves well, then set out on an enterprise about which they were warned by a friend: "It's the next thing to suicide."

That caution could not have been more wrong, for their journey took them into a natural wonderland where they met few Indians. From Bozeman, they traveled along the mountain range between the Gallatin and Yellowstone rivers, eventually crossing to the Yellowstone and ascending that river into the present park by way of Yankee Jim Canyon. They observed Tower Fall and nearby thermal features and the Grand Canyon of the Yellowstone—"this masterpiece of nature's handiwork"—then continued past the Mud Volcano to Yellowstone Lake. They pushed east to Mary Bay, then backtracked across the north shore to West Thumb. On their way home the explorers visited Shoshone Lake and the Lower and Midway Geyser Basins. The Folsom-Cook-Peterson exploration produced an updated version of deLacy's 1865 map, an article in the *Western Monthly* magazine in Chicago, and a fever of excitement among some of Montana's leading citizens, who promptly determined to see for themselves the truth of the party's tales of "the beautiful places we had found fashioned by the practised hand of nature, that man had not desecrated."

By August 1870 a second expedition had been organized. Rumors of Indian trouble reduced the original 20 members to fewer than half that number. Among them were prominent government officials and financial leaders of Montana Territory, led by Surveyor-General Henry D. Washburn, politician and business promoter Nathaniel P. Langford, and Cornelius Hedges, a lawyer. Obtaining from Fort Ellis a military escort under experienced soldier, Lt. Gustavus C. Doane, the explorers traced the general route of the 1869 party. They followed the river to the lake, passed around the eastern and southern sides, inspected the Upper, Midway, and Lower geyser basins, and paused at Madison Junction—the confluence of the Gibbon and Firehole rivers—before returning to Montana. It was at this campsite that they, like their predecessors the year before, discussed their hopes that Yellowstone might be saved from exploitation.

Some of the 1870 expedition lacked extensive experience as frontiersmen, and their wilderness education came hard. At time they went hungry because, according to Doane, "our party kept up such a rackett of yelling and firing as to drive off all game for miles ahead of us." One of their number, Truman Everts, separated himself from the rest of the party and, unable to subsist in a bounteous land, nearly starved to death before he was rescued 37 days later. But these problems were understandable. By the end of the expedition they had demonstrated their

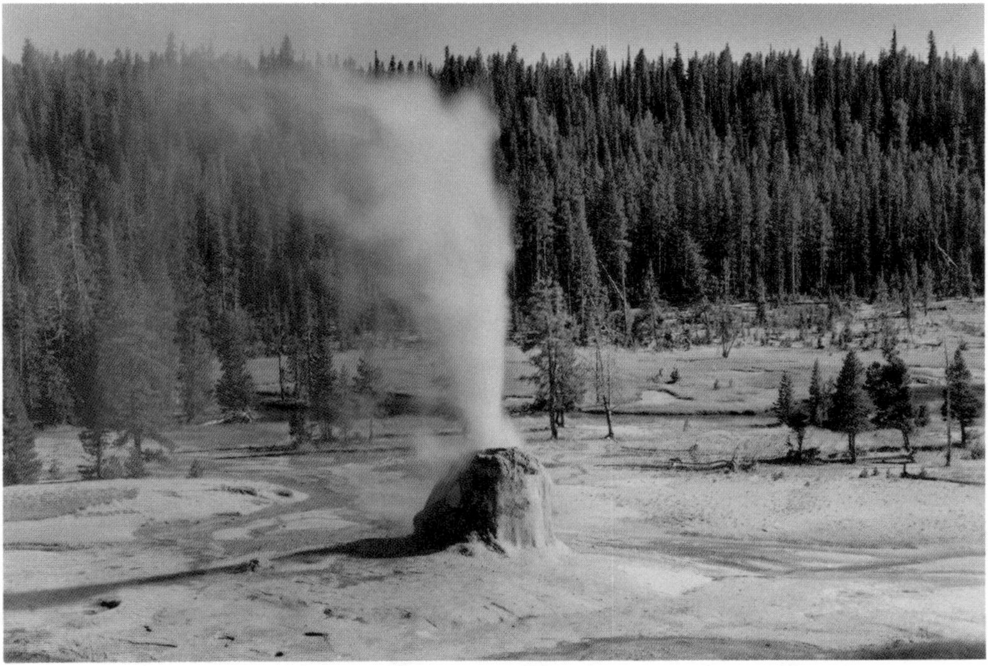

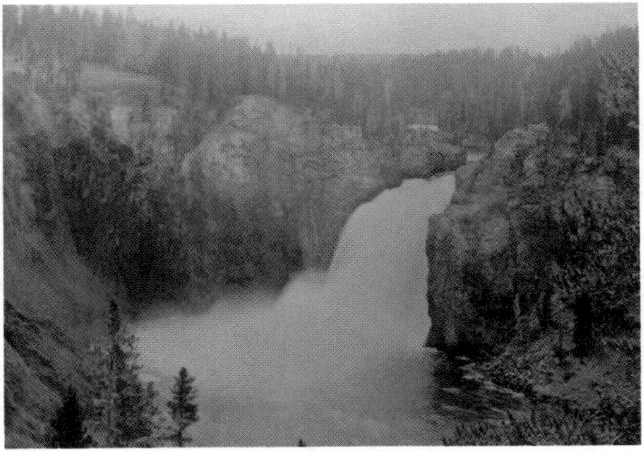

Three primary features were recognized as prominent evidence that this unique region merited protection. The geyser basins, (Lone Star Geyser, above), the Grand Canyon of the Yellowstone (Upper Falls, left) and Yellowstone Lake (head of Yellowstone Lake on the southeast arm, next page) were the three features enclosed in a square tract of land orginally encompassing approximately 3,348 square miles.

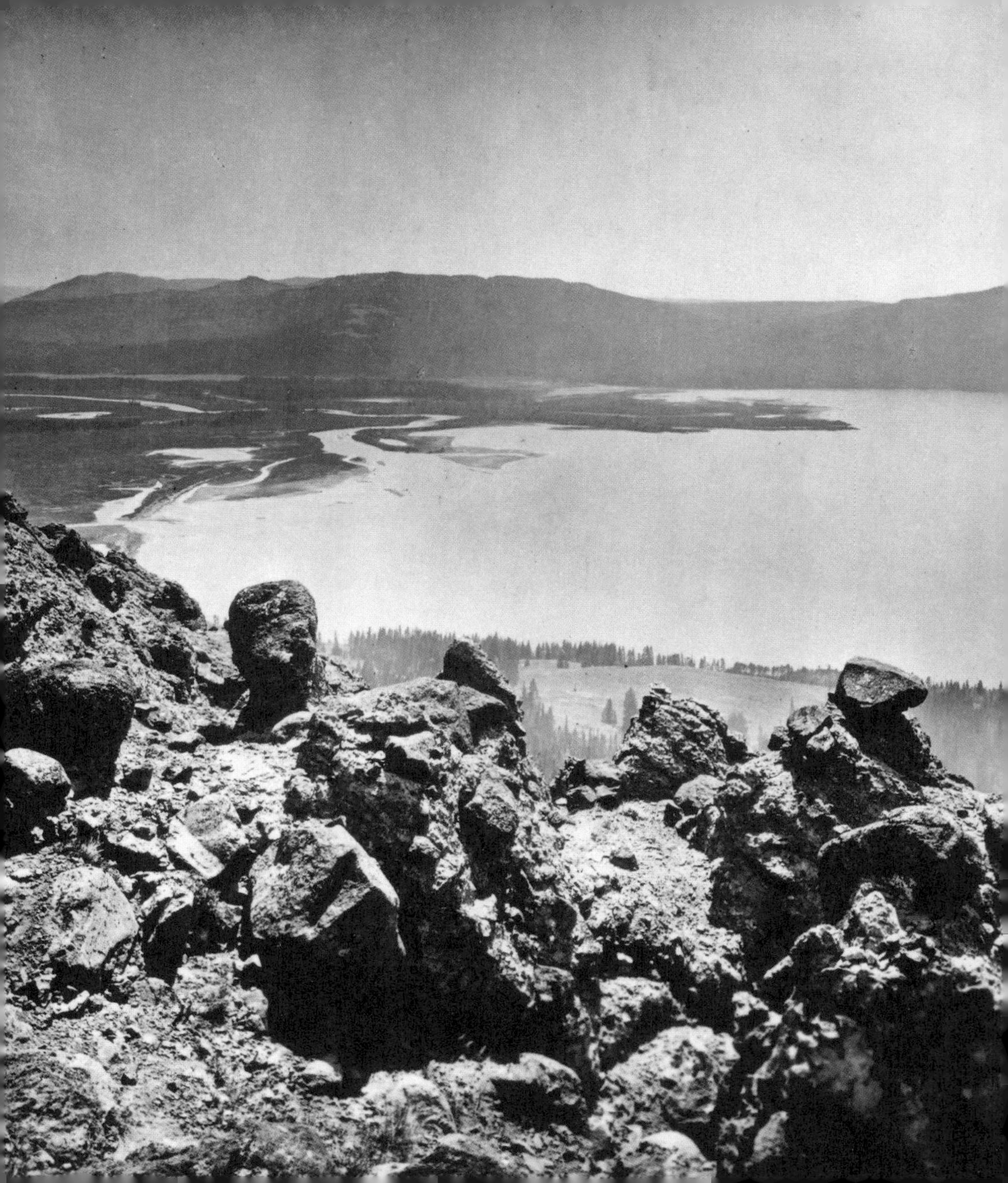

backwoods ability. The party had climbed several peaks, made numerous side trips, descended into the Grand Canyon of the Yellowstone, and attempted measurements and analyses of several of the prominent natural features. They had shown that ordinary men, as well as hardened frontiersmen, could venture into the wilderness of Yellowstone.

Far more important, however, was their enchantment and wonder at what they had seen and their success in publicizing these feelings. As Hedges later recalled, "I think a more confirmed set of sceptics never went out into the wilderness than those who composed our party, and never was a party more completely surprised and captivated with the wonders of nature." Their reports stirred intense interest in Montana and attracted national attention. Members of the expedition wrote articles for several newspapers and *Scribner's Monthly* magazine. Langford made a speaking tour in the East. Doane's official report was accepted and printed by the Congress. All this publicity resulted in a congressional appropriation for an official exploration of Yellowstone—the Hayden Expedition.

Ferdinand V. Hayden, physician turned geologist, energetic explorer and accomplished naturalist, head of the U.S. Geological Survey of the Territories, had been with Raynolds in 1860. The failure of that expedition to penetrate Yellowstone had stimulated his desire to investigate the region. Aside from being a leading scientific investigator of the wilderness, he was an influential publicist of the scientific wonders, scenic beauty, and economic potential of the American West. He saw the interest stirred by the Washburn-Langford-Doane Expedition as an opportunity to reveal Yellowstone in an orderly and scientific manner. Drawing on the support of the railroad interest—always proponents of Western exploration and development—and favorable public reaction to the reports of the 1870 expedition, Hayden secured an appropriation for a scientific survey of Yellowstone. This expedition was supplemented by a simultaneous survey by the U.S. Army Corps of Engineers.

The dual exploration in the late summer of 1871 was more than that of 1870, and it brought back scientific corroboration of earlier tales of thermal activity. Although a lot of the material vanished in the Chicago fire of 1871, the expedition gave the world a much improved map of Yellowstone and, in the excellent photographs by William Henry Jackson and the artwork of Henry W. Elliott and Thomas Moran, visual proof of Yellowstone's unique curiosities. The expedition's reports excited the scientific community and aroused intense national interest in this previously mysterious region.

Members of all three expeditions from 1869 to 1871 were overwhelmed by what they had seen. The singular features of the area evoked similar reactions in all the explorers. This was the day of the "robber barons" and of rapacious exploitation of the public domain. It was also a time of dynamic national expansion, when the nation conceived its mission to be the taming and peopling of the wilderness. But most of the region's explorers sensed that division and exploitation, through homesteading or other development, were not proper for Yellowstone. Its natural curiosities impressed them as being so valuable that the area should be reserved for all to see. Their crowning achievement was that they persuaded others to their view and helped to save Yellowstone from private development.

Hayden, assisted by members of the Washburn party and other interested persons, promoted a park bill in Washington in late 1871 and early 1872. Working earnestly, the sponsors drew upon the precedent of the Yosemite Act of 1864, which reserved Yosemite Valley from settlement and entrusted it to the care of the State of California, and the persuasive magic of Jackson's photographs, Moran's painting, and Elliott's sketches. Permanent closure to settlement of such an expanse of the public domain would be a departure from the established policy of transferring public lands to private ownership. But the proposed park encompassing the wonders of Yellowstone had caught the imagination of both the public and Congress. After some discussion but surprisingly little opposition, the measure passed both houses of Congress, and on March 1, 1872. President Ulysses S. Grant signed it into law. Yellowstone would be "dedicated and set apart as a public park or pleasuring-ground for the benefit and enjoyment of the people." The world's first national park was born.

"THE WILD ROMANTIC SCENERY"

Something about Yellowstone has frequently brought out the poet, or would-be poet, in its visitors. Men who ordinarily would not bother to remark on their surroundings have in Yellowstone felt compelled to draft prose about the wonders they saw around them. This impulse was particularly keen in those who saw Yellowstone before the advance of civilization.

Little is known of the Indian's regard for Yellowstone's natural features during the thousands of years they lived there. They did not leave their impressions in written form for the reflection of later generations.

But the fur trappers did. Several of them kept journals or related their experiences in letters and reminiscences. They used their observations to spin entertaining yarns, and sometimes compared the surrounding beauty with what they knew back home. Yet they generally resisted the "womanly emotions" of praising scenery, and most of them were reluctant to reflect on nature's charms. A Maine farm boy named Osborne Russell, who went West in the 1830s to trap, chided his companions for their insensitivity:

My comrades were men who never troubled themselves about vain and frivolous notions as they called them; with them every country was pretty when there was weather and as to beauty of nature or arts, it was all a "humbug" as one of them. . . often expressed it.

What Russell saw in Yellowstone affected him deeply. He had reverent memories of one place in particular, a "Secluded Valley," located on the Lamar River near the mouth of Soda Butte Creek.

There is something in the wild romantic scenery of this valley which I cannot describe; but the impressions made upon my mind while gazing from a high eminence on the surrounding landscape one evening as the sun was gently gliding behind the western mountain and casting its gigantic shadows across the vale were such as time can never efface from my memory. . . for my own part I almost wished I could spend the remainder of my days in a place like this where happiness and contentment seemed to reign in wild romantic splendor.

Thermal features drew the most frequent notice from Yellowstone's early visitors. Nathaniel Langford summarized the mystery and disbelief many people feel while observing them:

General Washburn and I again visited the mud vulcano [sic] to-day. I especially desired to see it again for the one especial purpose, among others of a general nature, of assuring myself that the notes made in my diary a few days ago are not exaggerated. No! they are not! The sensations inspired in me to-day, on again witnessing its convulsions. . . were those of mingled dread and wonder. At war with all former experience it was so novel, so unnaturally natural, that I feel while now writing and thinking of it, as if my own senses might have deceived me with a mere figment of the imagination.

But more often the hot springs, mud pots, fumaroles, and geysers seemed to suppress the poet and draw forth instead the amateur scientist. Most early accounts centered on attempts at measurement or analysis, or on speculations about the mechanisms of such features. For many of these novice geologists, the surprises at Yellowstone did not always come in the form of geysers or boiling springs. A. Bart Henderson, a prospector, was walking down the Yellowstone River in 1867, near the Upper Falls, when he was

very much surprised to see the water disappear from sight. I walked out on a rock & made two steps at the same time, one forward, the other backward, for I had unawares as it were, looked into the depth of bowels of the earth, into which the

Yellow[stone] plunged as if to cool the infernal region that lay under all this wonderful country of lava & boiling springs. The water fell several feet, struck a reef of rock that projected further than the main rock above. This reef caused the water to fall the remainder of the way in spray.

Henderson recovered his analytical composure and concluded, "We judged the falls to be 80 or 90 feet high, perhaps higher."

Because wildlife was plentiful everywhere in the West in the 19th century, the abundant wildlife of Yellowstone seldom drew the attention of early visitors, except when they referred to hunting the "wild game." Occasionally a diary registered that some physical feature had been endowed with the name of an animal. Prospector John C. Davis shot at what he thought was a flock of flying geese in 1864. But after a difficult swim to retrieve his prey, he decided that it was too strange to eat, and hung it in a tree. From that small incident Pelican Creek acquired its name.

Sometimes the wildlife forced their attentions on visitors. Henderson prospected in Yellowstone again in 1870. He christened Buffalo Flat because "we found thousands of buffalo quietly grazing." But the animals were evidently not flattered, for one night, "Buffalo bull run thro the tent, while all hands were in bed." As Henderson's party continued their journey, another bull attacked their horses, nearly destroying their sup-

Charles W. Cook

Nathaniel P. Langford, first superintendent of the park, 1872.

Truman C. Everts, alone and lost in the wilderness for 37 days.

plies. Sometime later, the group "met an old she bear & three cubs. After a severe fight killed the whole outfit, while a short distance further on we was attacked by an old boar bear. We soon killed him. He proved to be the largest ever killed in the mountains, weighing 960 pounds." Two days later, Henderson "was chased by an old she bear... Climbe[d] a tree & killed her under the tree."

But few encounters with wildlife were so unpleasant. Most travelers recognized that the animals of Yellowstone were an integral part of the environment. To David Folsom the voices of the animals were but the voice of nature, reminding men of their smallness in the natural world and of their aloneness in a strange country:

> *the wolf scents us afar and the mournful cadence of his howl adds to our sense of solitude. The roar of the mountain lion awakens the sleeping echoes of the adjacent cliffs and we hear the elk whistling in every direction. . . . Even the horses. . . stop grazing and raise their heads to listen, and then hover around our campfire as if their safety lay in our companionship.*

The explorers of 1869, 1870, and 1871, writing for a wide audience, did their best to remain detached and to describe objectively what they had seen. But their prose sometimes became impassioned. Even the thermal features evoked poetic word pictures. Charles Cook was startled by his first view of Great

/33

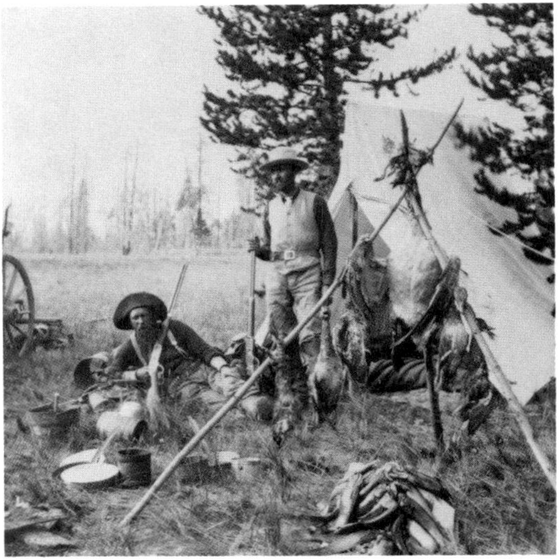

Early abuse of Yellowstone's wildlife. The trumpeter swan, ducks and fish (right) were brought in to satisfy a group camping on the shore of Yellowstone Lake in 1882. As wildlife began to diminish under the strain of over hunting, game corrals, bear and deer feeding (below) attempted to lure wildlife and people together.

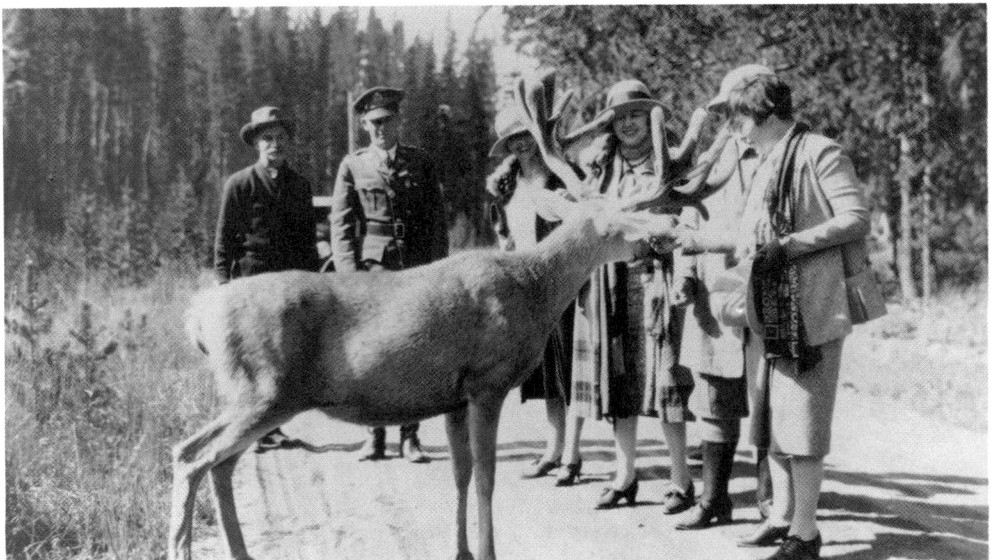

Fountain Geyser:
> Our attention was at once attracted by water and steam escaping, or being thrown up from an opening. . . . Soon this geyser was in full play. The setting sun shining into the spray and steam drifting toward the mountains, gave it the appearance of burnished gold, a wonderful sight. We could not contain our enthusiasm; with one accord we all took off our hats and yelled with all our might.

Folsom recalled his last look at Yellowstone Lake this way:
> nestled among the forest-crowned hills which bounded our vision, lay this inland sea, its crystal waves dancing and sparkling in the sunlight as if laughing with joy for their wild freedom. It is a scene of transcendent beauty which has been viewed by a few white men, and we felt glad to have looked upon it before its primeval solitude should be broken by the crowds of pleasure seekers which at no distant day will throng its shores.

Even the scientifically minded professional soldier, Gustavus Doane, departed from an objective recital to exclaim that the view from Mount Washburn was really "beyond all adequate description." Speaking of Tower Falls, Doane became cautiously lyrical:
> Nothing can be more chastely beautiful than this lovely cascade, hidden away in the dim light of overshadowing rocks and woods, its very voice hushed to a low murmur unheard at the distance of a few hundred yards. Thousands might pass by within a half mile and not dream of its existence, but once seen, it passes to the list of most pleasant memories.

The lieutenant dropped his reserve altogether when he sang the praises of the Upper and Lower Falls in the Grand Canyon of the Yellowstone:
> Both these cataracts deserve to be ranked among the great waterfalls of the continent. No adequate standard of comparison between such objects, either in beauty or grandeur, can well be obtained. Every great cascade has a language and an idea peculiarly its own, embodied, as it were, in the flow of its waters. . . . So the Upper Falls of the Yellowstone may be said to embody the idea of "Momentum," and the Lower Fall of "Gravitation." In scenic beauty the upper cataract far excels the lower; it has life, animation, while the lower one simply follows its channel; both however are eclipsed as it were by the singular wonders of the mighty cañon below.

The Hayden expeditions of 1871 and 1872 were scientific ventures, composed of men of critical disposition who were prepared to take a circumspect, unromantic

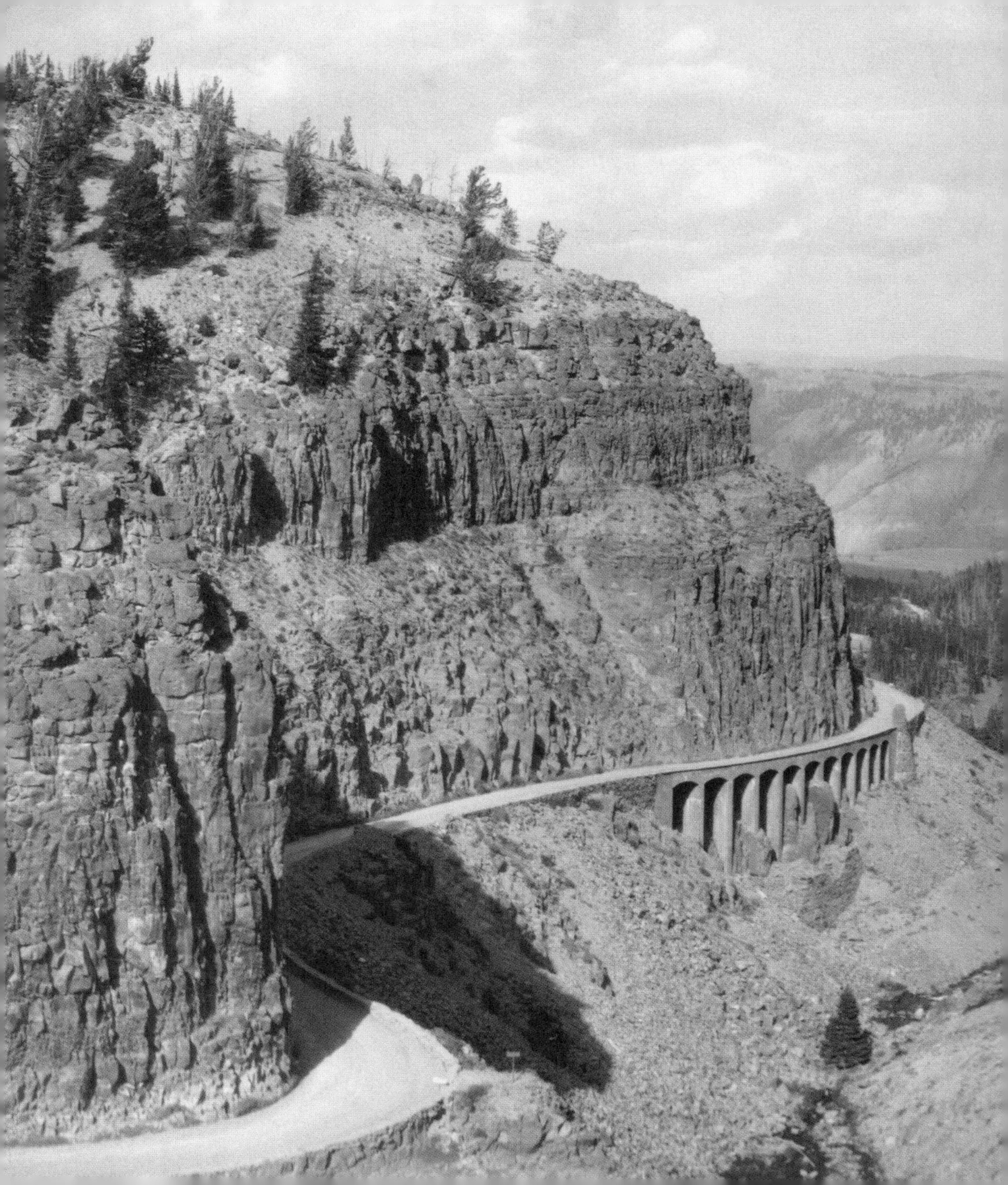

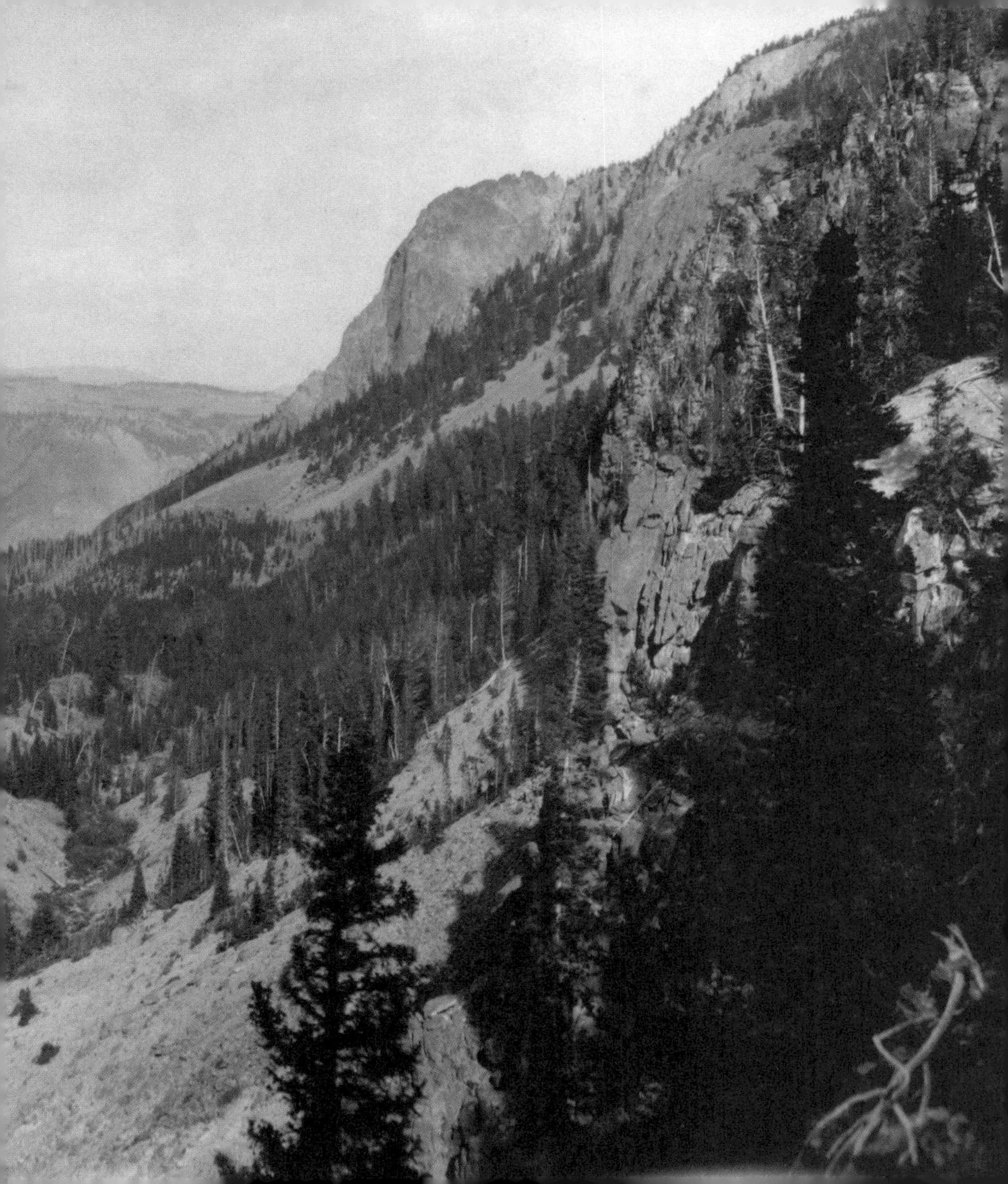

The U.S. Army administered Yellowstone during its early days from 1886 until 1918. The Army was responsible for constructing the figure-eight-shaped Grand Loop road and patroled from station to station by horseback, bicycle (above) and foot (at Yancy's Hole, right). Golden Gate (previous page), the first wooden bridge was originally built in 1884 prior to the Army and was later replaced with a concrete structure in 1901.

A soldier relaxes with his family at Fort Yellowstone, now called Mammoth.

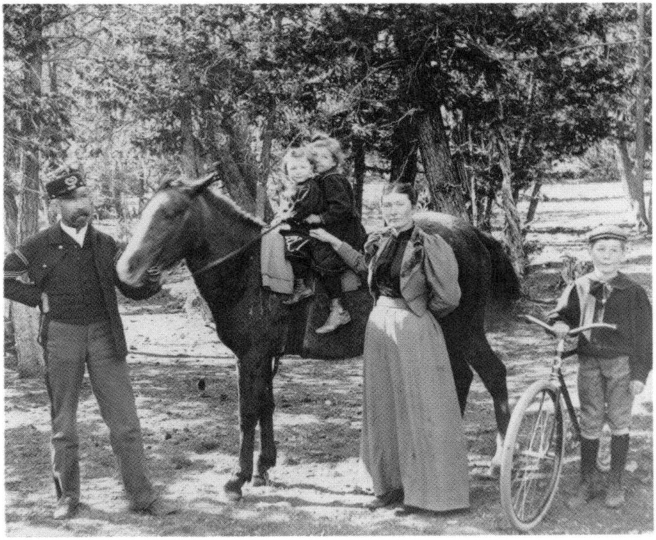

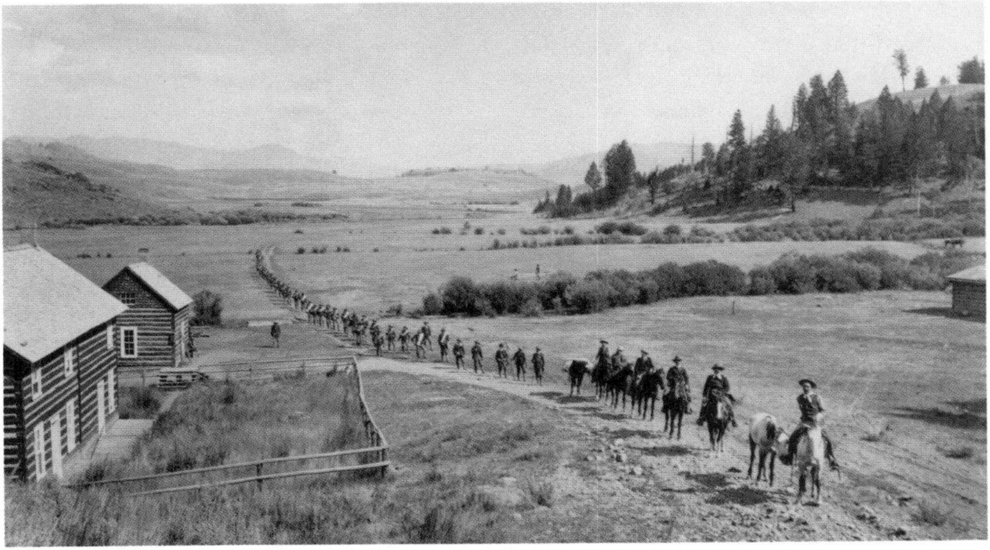

view of all they encountered in their path. Yet even they were moved to comment on the beauty of Yellowstone. Henry Gannett, one of Hayden's later associates, wrote:

> In one essential respect the scenery of the Yellowstone Park differs from that of nearly all other parts of the Cordilleras, in possessing the element of beauty, in presenting to the eye rounded forms, and soft, bright, gay coloring.

Nor could the scholarly Hayden completely restrict himself to scientific explanations of Yellowstone's charms. Mammoth Hot Springs, he thought, "alone surpassed all the descriptions which had been given by former travelers." When he came to the Grand Canyon and the falls, he confessed that mere description was inadequate, that "it is only through the eye that the mind can gather anything like an adequate conception of them":

> no language can do justice to the wonderful grandeur and beauty of the cañon below the Lower Falls; the very nearly vertical walls, slightly sloping down to the water's edge on either side, so that from the summit the river appears like a thread of silver foaming over its rocky bottom; the variegated colors of the sides, yellow, red, brown, white, all intermixed and shading into each other; the Gothic columns of every form standing out from the sides of the walls with greater variety and more striking colors than ever adorned a work of human art. The margins of the cañon on either side are beautifully fringed with pines. In some places the walls of the cañon are composed of massive basalt, so separated by the jointage as to look like irregular mason-work going to decay....
>
> Standing near the margin of the Lower Falls, and looking down the cañon, which looks like an immense chasm or cleft in the basalt, with its sides 1,200 to 1,500 feet high, and decorated with the most brilliant colors that the human eye ever saw, with the rocks weathered into an almost unlimited variety of forms, with here and there a pine sending its roots into the clefts on the sides as if struggling with a sort of uncertain success to maintain an existence—the whole presents a picture that it would be difficult to surpass in nature. Mr. Thomas Moran, a celebrated artist, and noted for his skill as a colorist, exclaimed with a kind of regretful enthusiasm that these beautiful tints were beyond the reach of human art.

Such were the men, from fur trappers to geologists, who preceded the civilized world into Yellowstone, and such were the feelings that nature produced in them. It was upon a stage thus set that Yellowstone entered into its greatest period—that of a wilderness preserved.

TO CONSERVE THE SCENERY AND OBJECTS THEREIN

The Yellowstone Park Act was essentially directed at preventing private ownership; it contained no revenues for administration of the preserve. The park's promoters envisioned that the Government would develop the park, and provide access by means of constructing roads. It was then hoped that the costs of maintenance and administration would be borne by fees charged at entrances and concessionaires, who would provide the facilities that the public needed. For a long time, therefore, Yellowstone enjoyed little protection from pillages.

One of the first needs was more thorough exploration. During the more than two decades following its establishment, a number of expeditions traversed much of the park and added greatly to the general store of knowledge. Especially notable were the elaborate Hayden Expedition of 1872 and a series of military explorations of the park later in the same decade. In 1883 an impressive bevy of scientists and celebrities escorted President Chester A. Arthur during what was more a pleasure trip than an exploration. By the early 1890s the park was well mapped, most of its features had been recorded, and it had even been penetrated during the bitter winters.

But the emerging park soon faced a new set of problems. Squatters had already moved in, and vandals and poachers preyed on its natural wealth. No congressional appropriation provided for protection or administration.

The Secretary of the Interior did, however, appoint a superintendent. In May 1872 this honor fell to Nathaniel P. Langford, member of the Washburn Expedition and advocate of the Yellowstone Park Act. Receiving no salary, he had to earn his living elsewhere and entered the park only twice during his 5 years in office, one in the train of the 1872 Hayden Expedition and again in 1874 to evict a particularly egregious squatter. When he was there, his task was made more difficult by the lack of statutory protection for wildlife and other natural features.

Because there were no appropriations for administration or improved access, the park remained inaccessible to all but the hardiest travelers. Some of the visitors who did make their way to the neglected paradise displayed a marked propensity to go about, according to an observer, "with shovel and axe, chopping and hacking and prying up great pieces of the most ornamental work they could find." In 1874 a Montana newspaper queried: "What has the Government done to render this national elephant approachable and attractive since its adoption as one of the nation's pets? Nothing." Langford complained, "Our Government, having adopted it, should foster it and render it accessible to the people of all lands, who in future time will come in crowds to visit it."

/41

Political pressure stemming partly from accusations of neglect of duty forced Langford's removal from the superintendency in April 1877. He was replaced by Philetus W. Norris, a hyper-energetic pioneer of quite a different stamp. Shortly after taking office, Norris became the regular recipient of an annual salary and appropriations "to protect, preserve, and improve the Park." Bringing skill and industry to the task, he constructed numerous physical improvements, built a monumental "blockhouse" on Capitol Hill at Mammoth Hot Springs for use as park headquarters, hired the first "gamekeepeer" (Harry Yount, an experienced frontiersman), and waged a difficult campaign against poachers and vandals. Much of the primitive road system he laid out still endures as part of the Grand Loop. Through ceaseless exploration and identification of the physical features, Norris added immensely to the geographical knowledge of the park. In this effort he left a prominent legacy, for among the names he liberally bestowed on the landscape, his own appeared frequently. One visitor felt he was "simply paying a visit to 'Norris' Park." Another caustically suggested:

Take the Norris wagon road and follow down the Norris fork of the Firehole River to the Norris Canyon of the Norris Obsidian Mountain; then go on to Mount Norris, on the summit of which you find. . . the Norris Blowout, and at its northerly base the Norris Basin and Park. Further on you will come to the Norris Geyser plateau, and must not fail to see Geyser Norris.

Despite the physical improvement he made in the park and his contributions to scientific knowledge, Norris fell victim to political machinations and was removed from his post in February 1882. As the ax fell, a Montana newspaper lamented:

We are led to infer that Peterfunk Windy Norris' cake is dough; in other words he has gone where the woodbine twineth; or to speak plainly, he has received the grand bounce. It is extremely sad. . . We shall never look upon [his] like again.

The removal of Norris was indicative of Yellowstone's plight. During its formative years, the park was fought over by interests that for political or financial reasons hoped to claim it as a prize and control it totally. Without legal protection against such exploitation or against poaching and vandalism, the park suffered greatly during its first two decades. An active and conscientious, if abrasive, superintendent like Norris was unable to fully protect the park. After his dismissal, promoters of schemes to build railroads and toll roads in the park and to monopolize accommodations usually blocked the appointment of capable superintendents and harassed any who showed signs of honestly striving for the benefit of the park. A succession of powerless and mediocre superintendents took

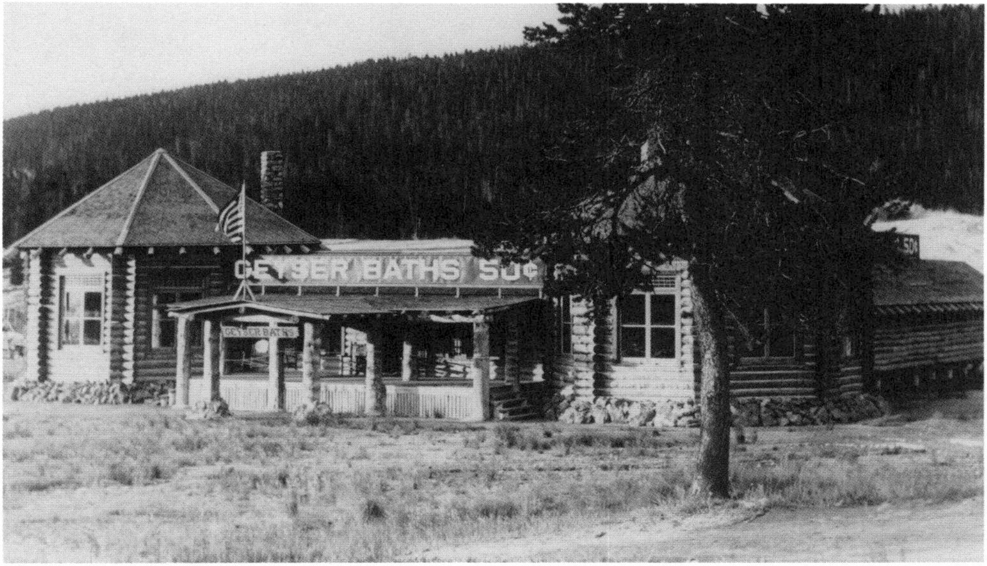
GEYSER BATHS 50¢
GEYSER BATHS

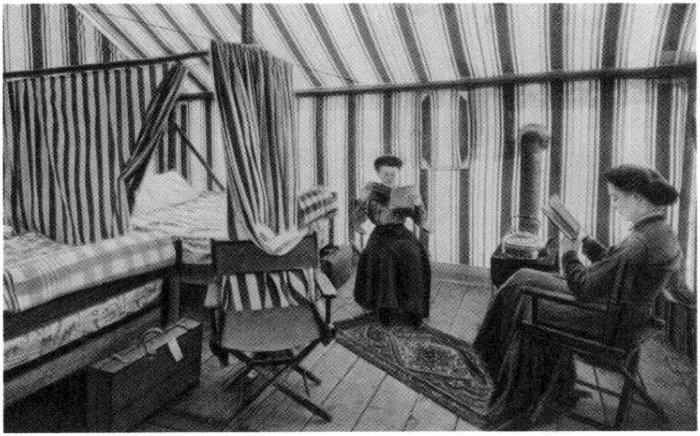

Hot Baths and luxurious Wylie Tent Camps greeted dudes and sagebrushers who arrived at Old Faithful during their Grand Loop tour of the Park.

This group appears excited about clean linen. The famous Handkerchief Pool was once the drawing attraction to Black Sand Basin, where tourists dropped their handkerchiefs into this small spring. Convection currents then whisked their laundry away after which it would reappear at the surface, freshly laundered.

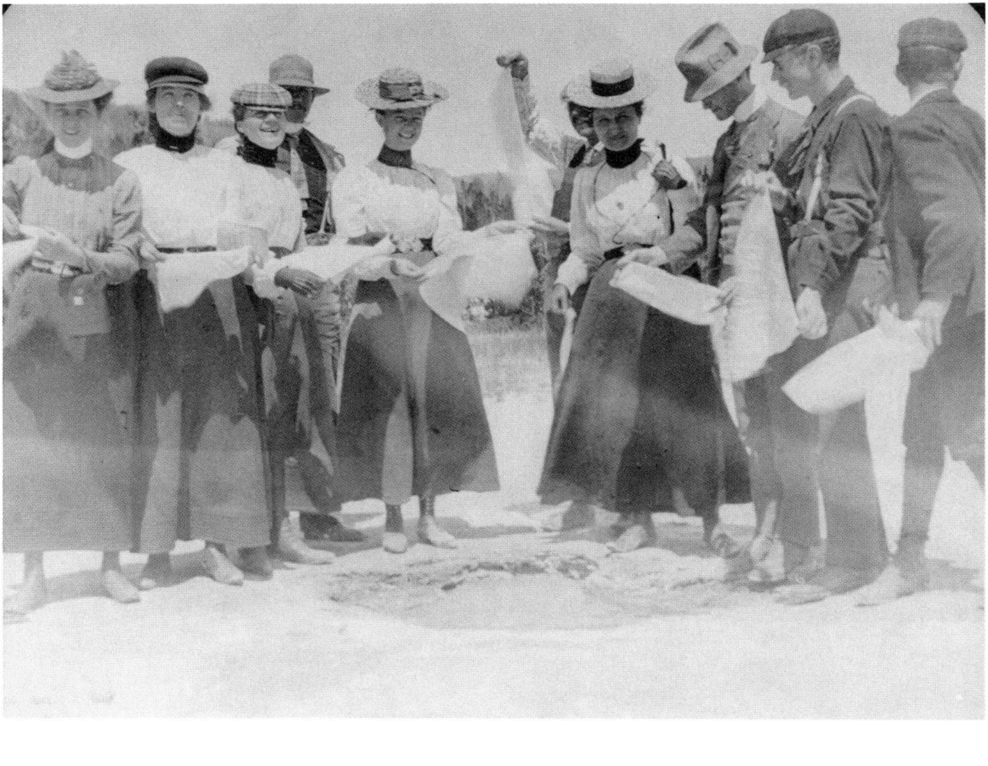

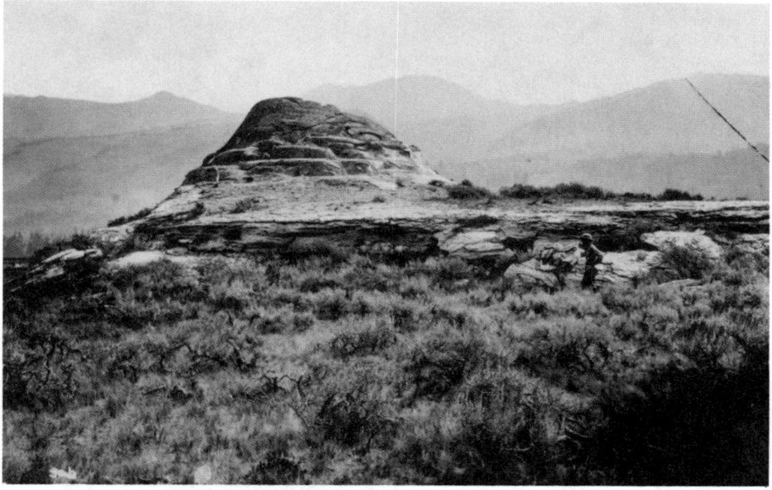

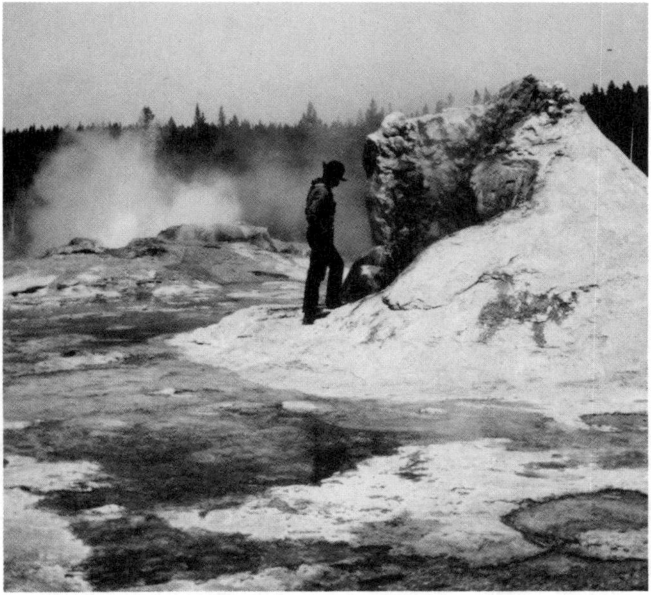

Thermal springs and geysers captivated early explorers and visitors, and to discover a "new" one was always a delight, even though it might be an extinct cone, like Soda Butte (above), or an old geyser, like Giant Geyser (left).

The chasm of the Grand Canyon of the Yellowstone (next page).

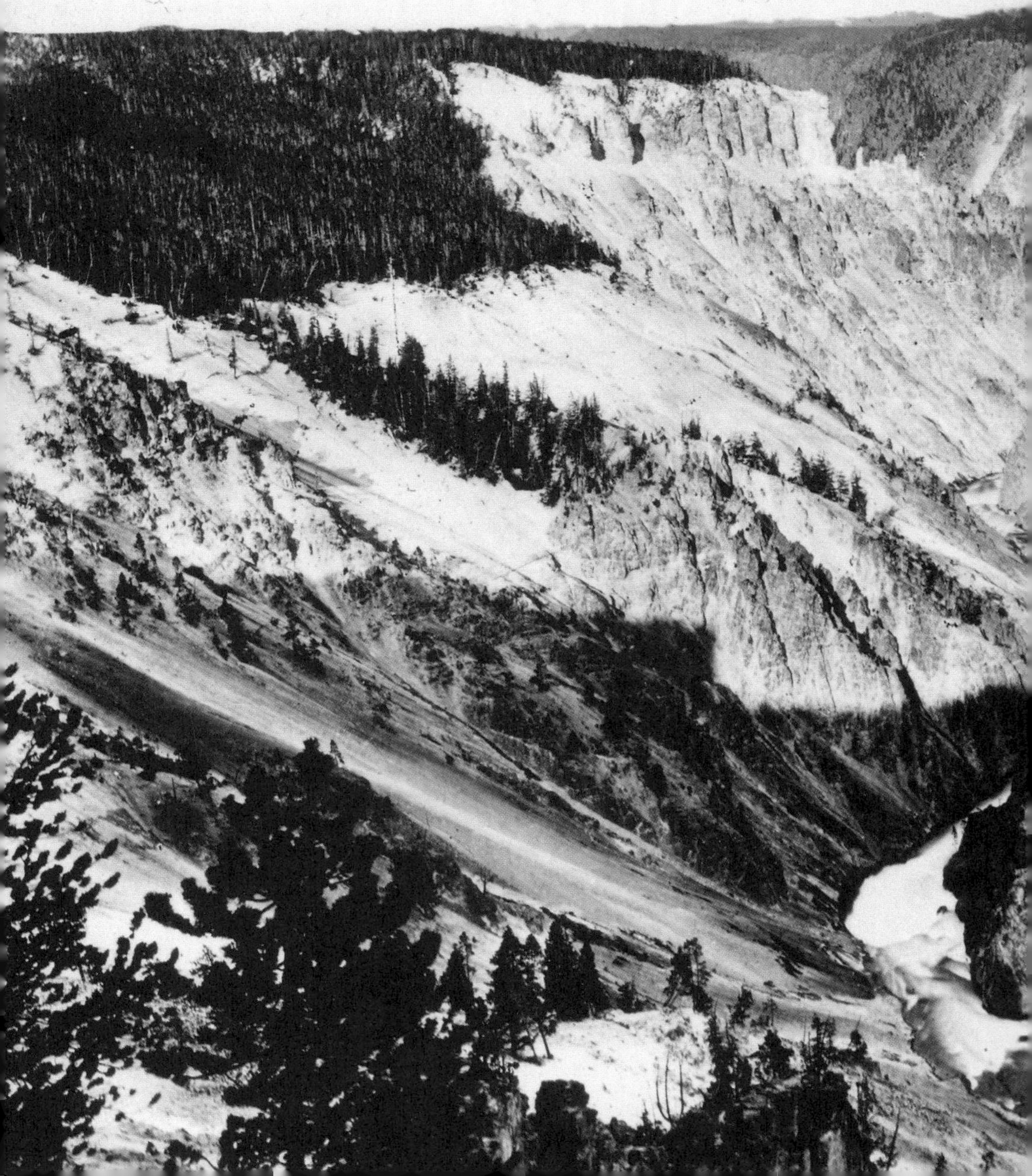

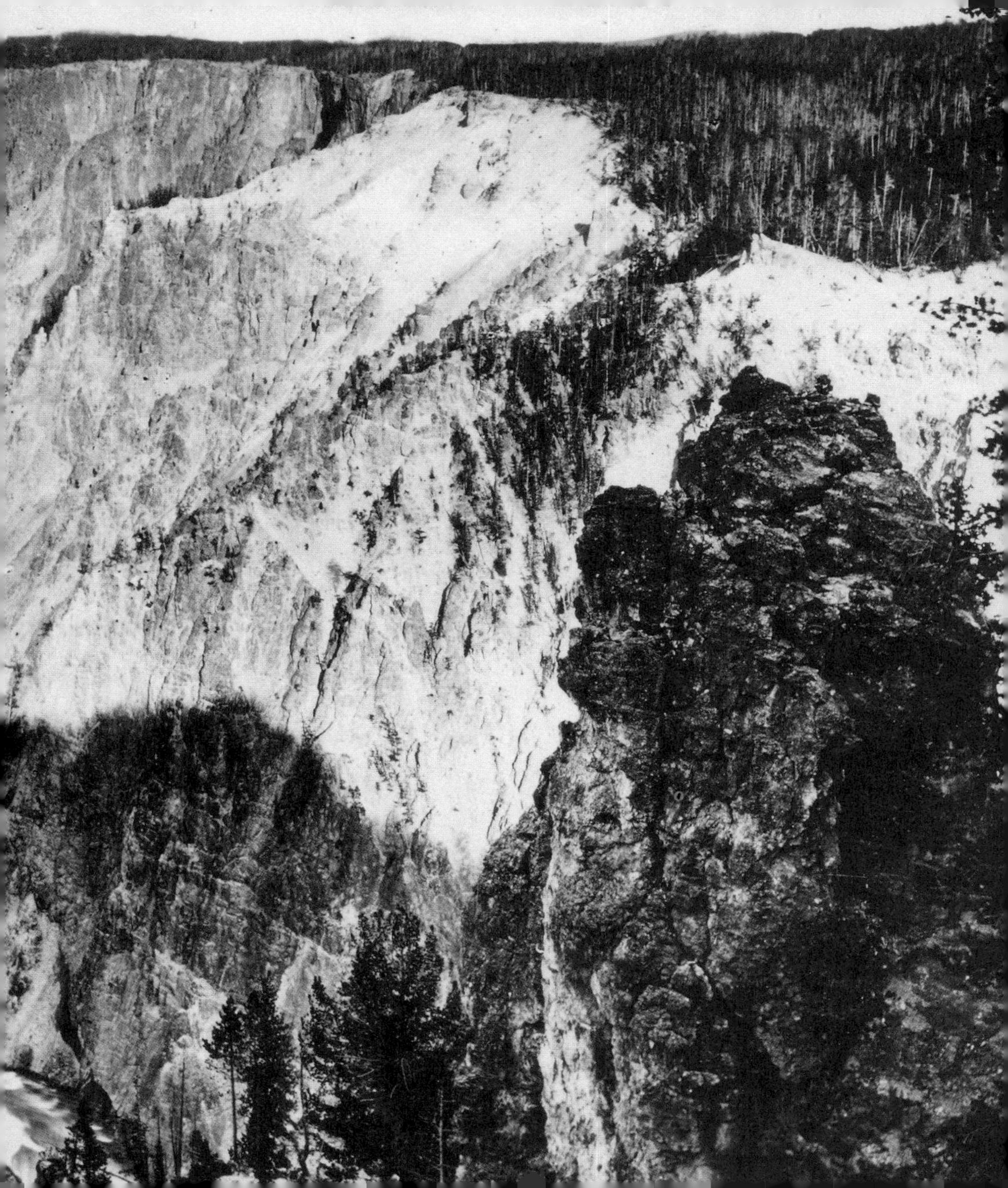

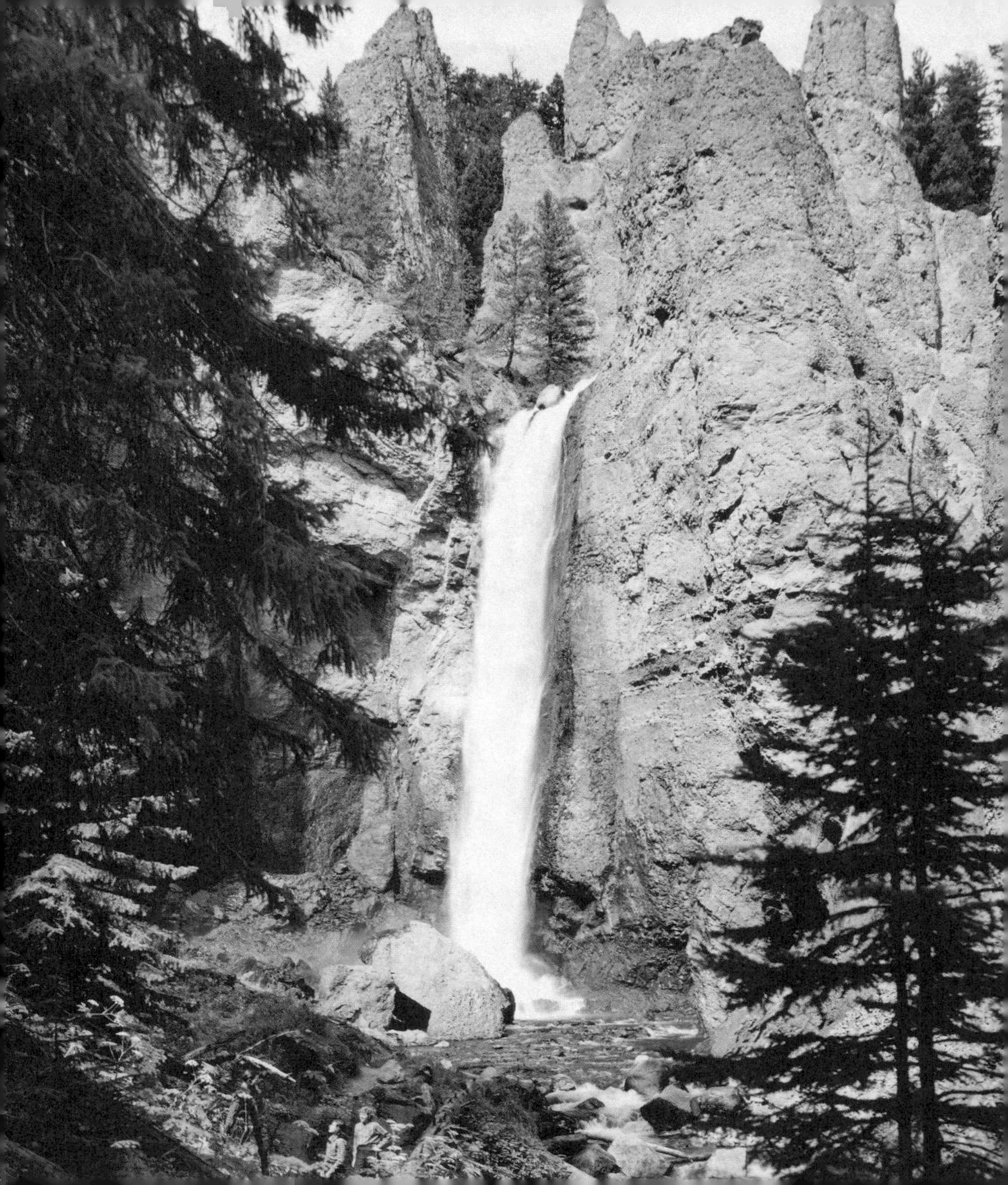

office. Of one of them it was remarked:

> *It need only be said that his administration was throughout characterized by a weakness and inefficiency which brought the Park to the lowest ebb of its fortunes, and drew forth the severe condemnation of visitors and public officials alike.*

It should be pointed out, however, that the national park was a totally new invention. No one had experience in the administration of such a preserve, and a long period of trial and error was bound to follow its establishment. The legal responsibilities of the Government were not full recognized, for it was commonly believed that the public could best be served and the park best be protected by concessioners. Yet it was difficult to distinguish the honest concessioner from the exploiter, to determine what kind of legal protection would best serve the common good, and to identify those human activities detrimental to the park. The isolation of Yellowstone compounded these handicaps. Although some visitors were destructive and a few rapacious exploiters wielded enormous influence, the Government was honestly striving to find the proper course in a new enterprise. Fortunately, most early visitors restricted their activities to the peaceful enjoyment of Yellowstone's wonders.

Attempts were made in the early 1880s to bring law and order to Yellowstone. A body of 10 assistant superintendents was created to act as a police force. Described by some observers as "notoriously inefficient if not positively corrupt" and scorned a "rabbit catchers" by Montana newspapers, they failed to check the rising tide of destruction and the slaughter of game. For two years the laws of Wyoming Territory were extended into the park, but the practice of enforcement that allowed "informers" and magistrates to split the fines degraded the hoped-for protection almost to the level of extortion. After the repeal of the act authorizing such "protection" was announced in March 1886, the obviously defenseless park attracted a new plague of poachers, squatters, woodcutters, vandals, and firebugs.

The inability of the superintendents to protect the park appeared to be a failure to perform their duty, and in 1886 Congress refused to appropriate money for such ineffective administration. Since no superintendent was willing to serve without pay, Yellowstone now lacked even the pretense of protection.

This circumstance proved fortunate, for the Secretary of the Interior, under authority previously given by the Congress, called on the Secretary of War for assistance. After August 20, 1886, Yellowstone came under the care of men not obliged to clamor for the job, and whose careers depended on performance—soldiers of the U.S. Army.

Military administration greatly benefited Yellowstone. Regulations were revised and conspicuously posted around the park, and patrols enforced them constantly. For the protection of visitors, as well as park features, detachments guarded the major attractions. No law spelled out offenses, but the Army handled problems effectively by evicting troublemakers and forbidding their return. Cavalry, better suited than infantry to patrol its vastness, usually guarded the park.

When appropriations for improvements increased, the Corps of Engineers lent its talents to converting the primitive road network into a system of roads and trails that in basic outline still endures. The soldier who left the greatest mark on Yellowstone was one of the engineers, Hiram M. Chittenden. He not only supervised much of its development and constructed the great arch at the northern entrance, but also wrote the first history of the park.

Army headquarters was at Mammoth Hot Spring, first in Camp Sheridan and after the 1890s in Fort Yellowstone, which still houses the park headquarters. A scattering of "soldier stations" around the park served as subposts. One survives today at Norris.

The most persistent menace to the park came from poachers. Although these intruders never killed any defender of the park—there was only one shoot-out with poachers in more than 30 years—their ceaseless attempts to make petty gains from the wildlife threatened to exterminate some animals. In 1894, soldiers arrested a man named Ed Howell for slaughtering bison and took him to Mammoth. The presence there of Emerson Hough, a prominent journalist, helped to generate national interest in the problem. Within two months Congress had acted, and the National Park Protective Act (Lacey Act) became law, finally providing teeth for the protection of Yellowstone's treasures. Howell entered the park that year to continue his bloody pastime. Appropriately, he became the first person arrested and punished under the new law.

The Army compiled an admirable record during its three decades of administration. But, running a park was not the Army's usual line of work. The troops could protect the park and ensure access, but they could not fully satisfy the visitor's desire for knowledge. Moreover, each of the 14 other national parks established during this period was separately administered, resulting in uneven management, inefficiency, and a great lack of direction.

It was generally agreed by 1916 that the national parks needed separate administration attuned to the special requirements of such preserves. The creation of the National Park Service that year eventually gave the parks their own force of men who were ordered by the Congress "to conserve the scenery and the natural and historic objects and the wild life therein and to provide for the enjoyment of the same in such manner and by such means as will leave them unimpaired

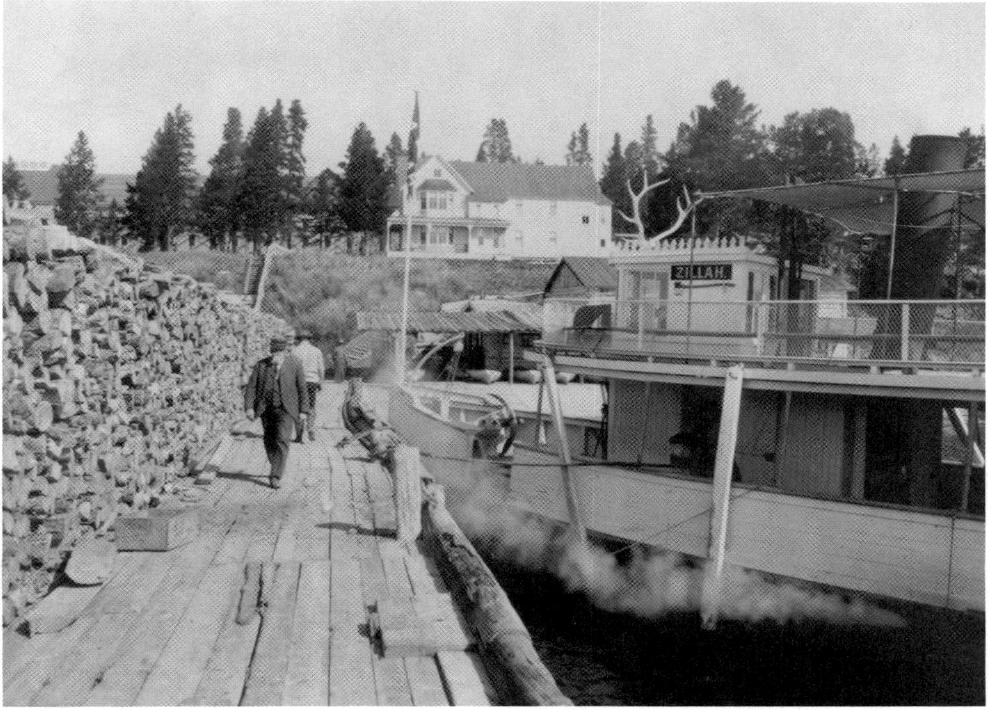
ZILLAH.

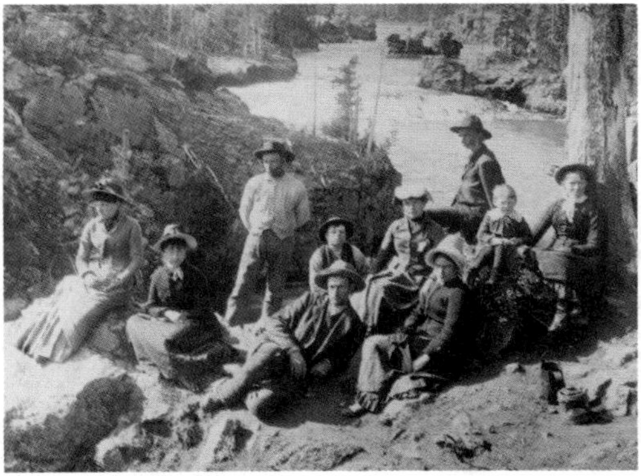

The steamer Zillah (above) was one of the first of many tour boats that have plied Yellowstone Lake. Tourists who stayed at Lake Hotel (next page) could tour Yellowstone Lake aboard the Zillah or continue their journey on the Grand Tour and overlook the brink of the Upper Falls of the Yellowstone River.

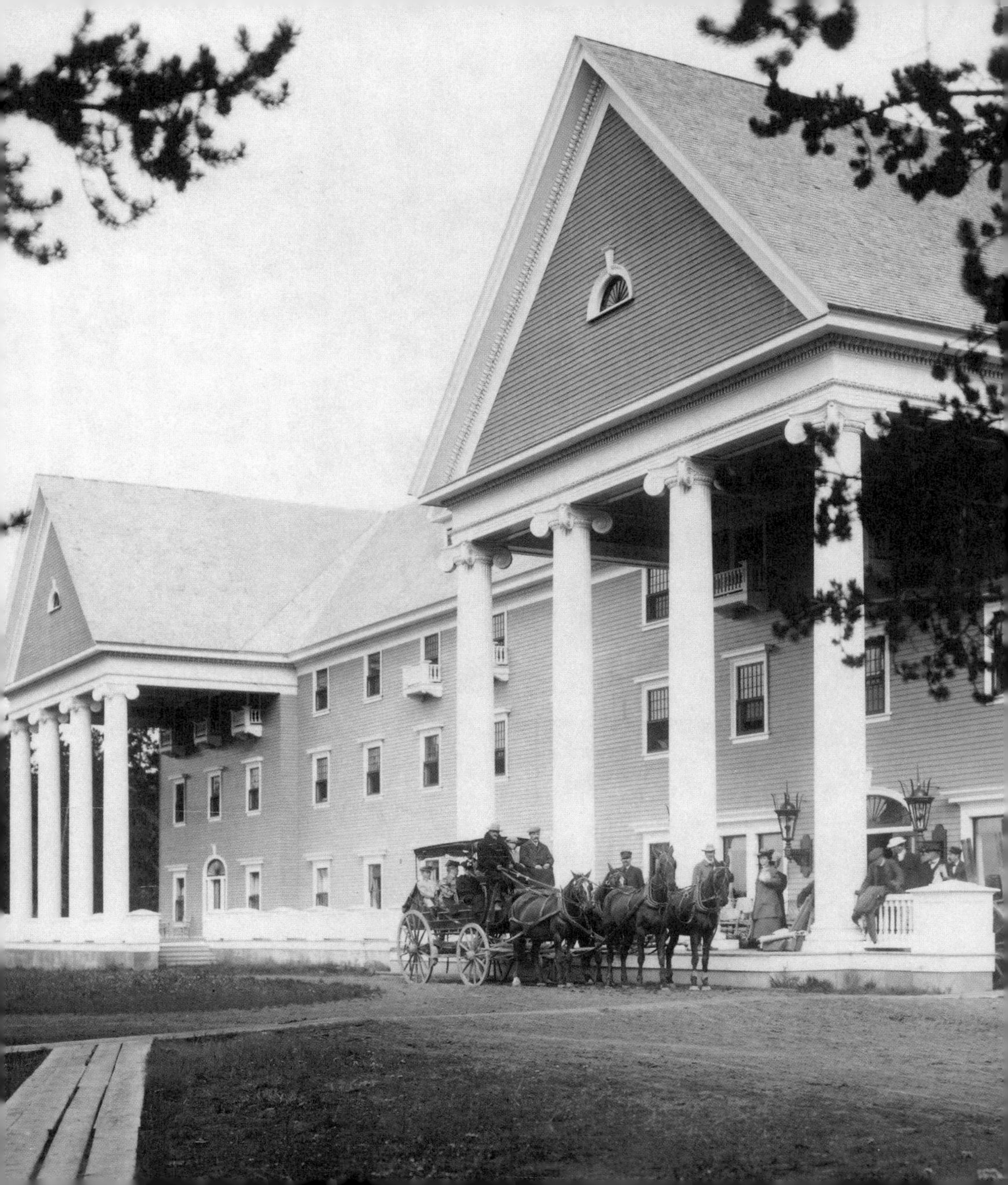

for the enjoyment of future generations."

A Park Service ranger force, including several veterans of the Army service in the park, assumed responsibility for Yellowstone in 1918. Protection was complicated now by the growing number of visitors that toured the park in automobiles. The influx of cars meant that in time roles changed and shifted to meet the changing world outside the boundaries of the park.

The appointment of Horace M. Albright to the post of superintendent in 1919 portended a broader approach to the management of the park than just protection of its features. Serving simultaneously in that office and as assistant to Stephen T. Mather, the Director of the National Park Service, Albright established a tradition of thoughtful administration that gave vitality and direction to the management of Yellowstone for decades. In 1929 he succeeded Mather as Director.

The 1920s and 30s brought development to Yellowstone in the form of government aid programs. The Civilian Conservation Corps (CCC) provided through strenuous physical work, roads, bridges and trails. Trailside museums, gifts of the Laura Spellman Rockefeller Foundation, supplemented these services. Eventually, as the needs of the public grew, programs became more extensive as hotels and services met the demands of increasing visitation.

Also during the 1920s and early 30s the park's boundaries were adjusted. An offshoot of the boundary revision campaign was the establishment of Grand Teton National Park to protect the magnificent Teton Range—a movement in which the superintendent of Yellowstone, Horace Albright, and industrialist, John D. Rockefeller, played crucial roles.

TOURING THE PARK

The experience of tourists in Yellowstone before the days of the family automobile was quite unlike that of modern visitors. The natural features that have always attracted people to the park appear much the same today, but the manner of travelling to the park and making the Grand Tour in the early days would now seem utterly foreign. "The old Yellowstone—the Yellowstone of the pioneer and the explorer—is a thing of the past," wrote Chittenden after automobiles gained access in 1915.

> *To the survivors, now grown old, of the romantic era of the park who reveled in the luxury of "new" things, who really felt as they wandered through this fascinating region that they were treading virgin soil, who traveled on foot or horseback and slept only in tents or beneath the open sky—to them the park means something which it does not mean to the present-day visitor. And that is why these old-timers as a rule have ceased to visit the park. The change saddens them, and they prefer to see the*

region as it exists in memory rather than in its modern reality.

One of the greatest attractions of old Yellowstone was the opportunity to bathe in the hot springs. In a day when a hot bath was a luxury and people were less sophisticated about their medical needs, hot mineral baths were popularly believed to have curative powers—not to mention the simple pleasure of soaking in hot water. Hot springs around the world enjoyed long careers as "spas" for the well-to-do and resorts for health seekers. And it was the hot waters of Yellowstone that attracted many of its first pleasure-seekers. In July 1872, while the second Hayden Expedition was exploring the park, a crowd of at least 50 people enjoyed the waters of Mammoth Hot Springs and the delights of James McCartney's hotel—really a log shack—and ramshackle bathhouse—in actuality a set of flimsy tents sheltering water-filled hollows in the ground. Gen. John Gibbon patronized the establishment in 1872 and left a record of this peculiar form of pleasure:

Already, these different bathhouses have established a local reputation with reference to their curative qualities. Should you require parboiling for rheumatism, take No. 1; if a less degree of heat will suit your disease, and you do not care to lose all your cuticle, take No. 2. Not being possessed of any disease I chose No. 3, and took one bath—no more.

McCartney's facilities became somewhat more comfortable, then passed from the scene, but other such resorts appeared throughout the park. Bathhouse enterprises, offering springs of various temperatures and presumed possessing medicinal powers, sprouted in the several thermal areas. They enjoyed a brisk business well into the 20th century, when changing modes of leisure reduced their popularity.

Fewer than 500 people a year came to Yellowstone before 1877, but thereafter the number of visitors increased steadily. Getting there in the first few years was a great problem. Tourists either transported themselves or patronized one or more of the intermittent transportation enterprises that carted them from Montana towns to the park. Once in the park they were on their own, finding sustenance during the early years only from a few concessioners or squatters who provided rude fare and minimal sleeping accommodations. Some early tourists were wealthy aristocrats, including a few titled Europeans who came well prepared to tour in grand style. But most of the earlier visitors were frontier people accustomed to roughing it—and they had to.

During the 1880s a visit to Yellowstone became easier. Access improved as the Northern Pacific Railroad reached Gardiner, on the north edge of the park. The Bozeman Toll Road Company, later known as the Yankee Jim Toll Road in honor of its colorful owner,

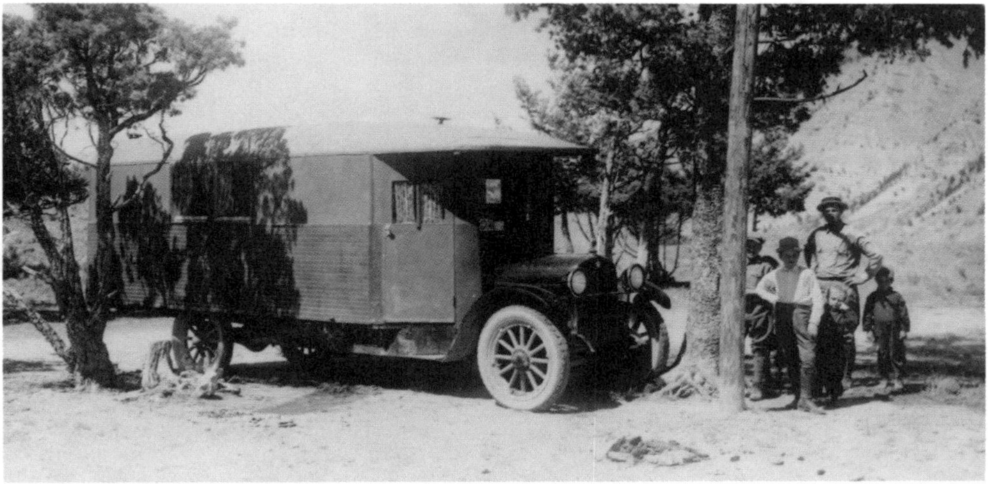

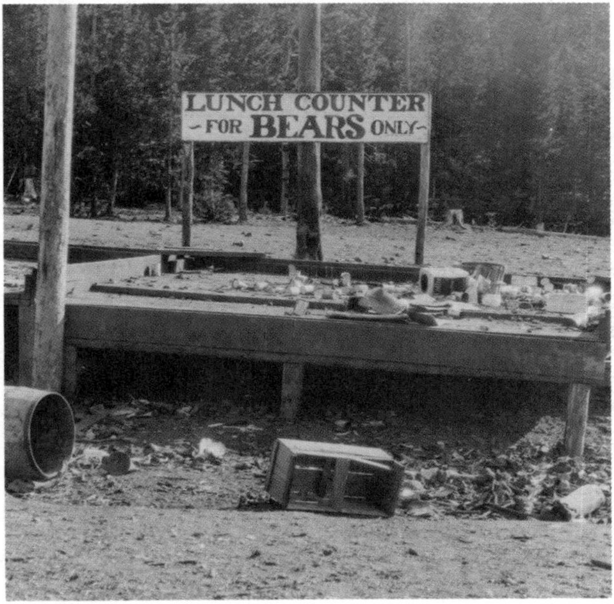
LUNCH COUNTER
FOR BEARS ONLY

After the advent of the automobile, different forms of transportation began bringing visitors to Yellowstone.

Bears and Yellowstone have gone hand in hand. To bring the elusive and shy bear out of the forest and into the open for public observation, rangers once staged public feeding counters and daily shows before a grandstand audience.

Old Faithful Inn (next page) has greeted travel-weary visitors with a warm reception since it was constructed during the winter of 1903-1904.

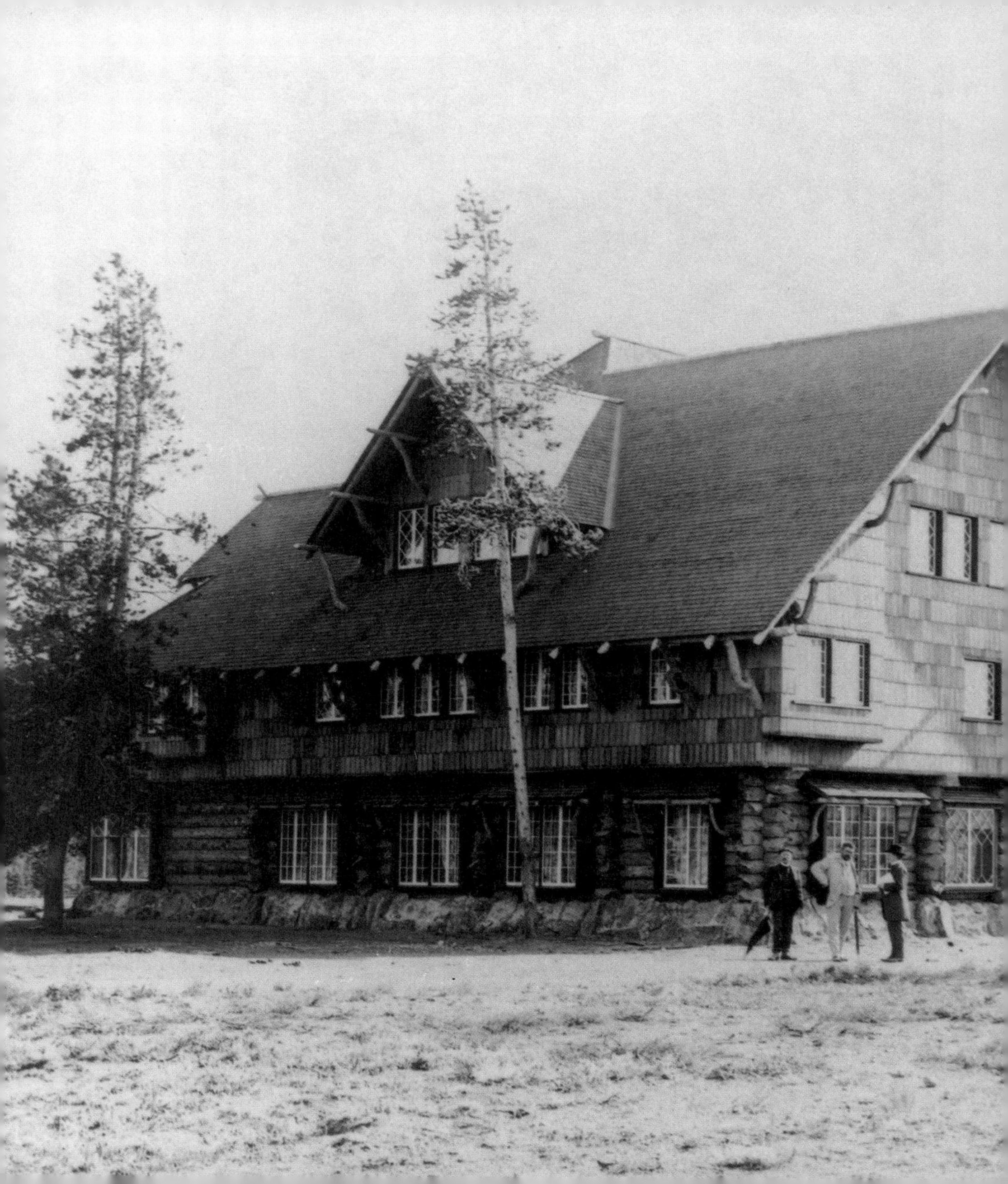

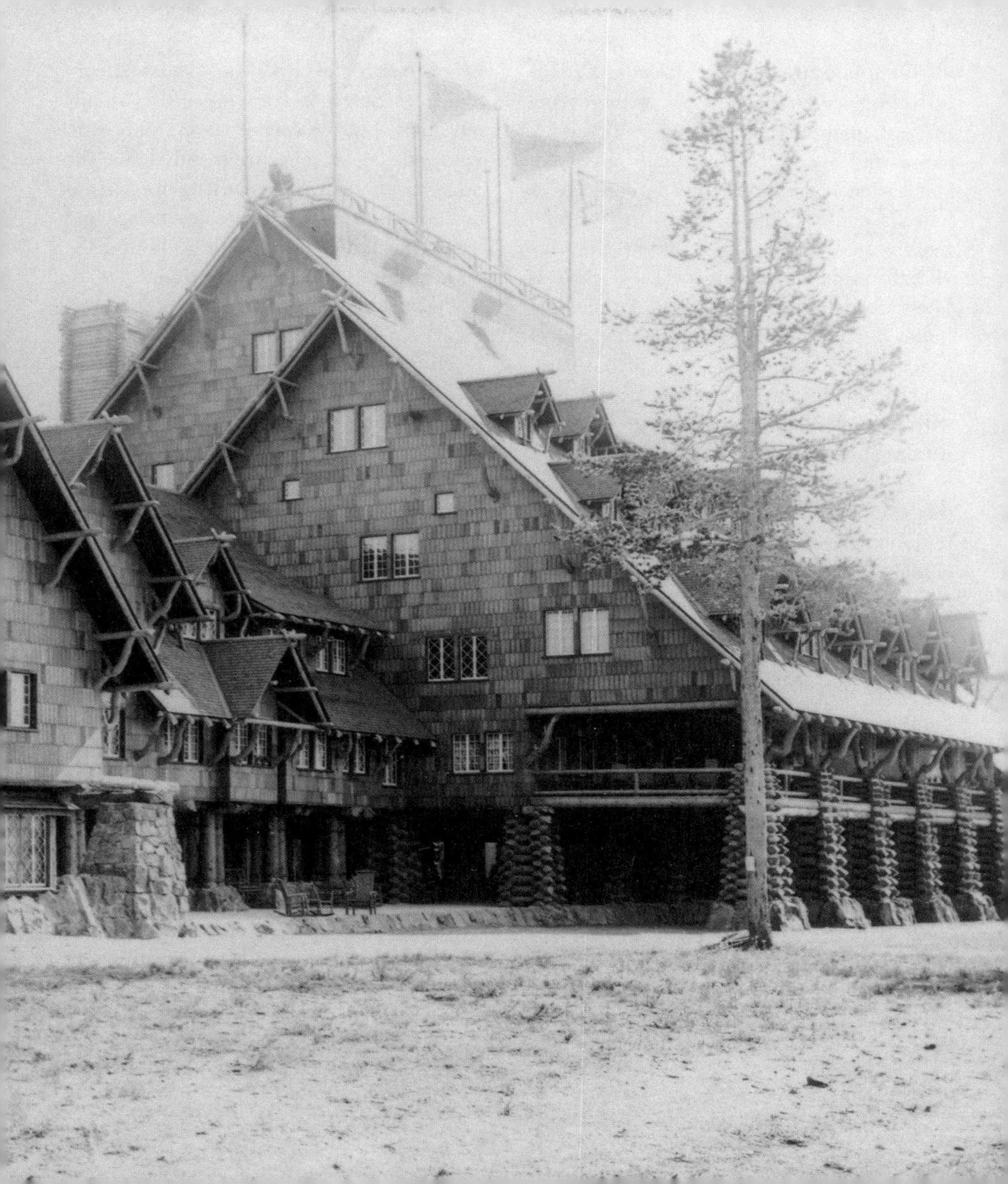

also facilitated travel. The railroads, particularly the Northern Pacific, took an increasing interest in the tourist business of Yellowstone and were the financial angels of concessioner operations. After the early 1880s tourists could step down from a Northern Pacific train, and as part of a ticket package visit the prominent features of the park. Yellowstone acquired a number of the large hotels popular as resorts in that day. Stagecoaches took visitors on tours of the park, usually on a five-day schedule. For the man with money, Yellowstone soon became rewarding and enjoyable place for a vacation.

Yellowstone was not yet a park for all of the people. Because of the expense of transportation in the late 19th and early 20th centuries, the travel industry in general was patronized mainly by the upper middle class—the affluent leaders of the industrial revolution. People accustomed to spending summers in Europe or at rich resorts like Saratoga Springs, N.Y., were the principal patrons of the Yellowstone package tours and "See America First" campaigns of the railroads. Though some people of lesser means did visit Yellowstone in the stagecoach days, the concessioners were dependent mainly on the "carriage trade." The difficulty of crosscountry transportation and the expense of such a vacation for many years put the enjoyment of Yellowstone's wonders out of reach for those who could not go first class.

Even wealthy tourists—"dudes" as they were called in the park—faced a few inconveniences. Stagecoach travel could be bumpy and dusty, but the scenery more than compensated. The coaches frequently had to be unloaded at steep grades, giving the passengers an opportunity to stretch their legs and breathe in the cool air while following the vehicles uphill. Stagecoach accidents were a rare possibility. And, of course, there were a few holdups.

Despite the attention the popular press gave to robberies, there were only five stagecoach holdups in the park—four of them involving coaches on the Grand Tour. The second, in 1908, was the most impressive of the 20th century; in a single holdup one enterprising bandit fleeced 174 passengers riding 17 stagecoaches. Despite their cash loss, holdup victims were entranced with their robbers, for some were entertaining fellows who never seriously hurt the well-heeled "dudes." A holdup was an added bit of excitement to an already enjoyable tour. As one tourist remarked, "We think we got off cheap and would sell our experience, if we could, for what it cost us."

Most tourists and visitors to the park exhibited that attitude. The minor inconvenience could not combine to eliminate the pleasure of "doing Yellowstone" in style. Mingling with their own kind, breathing an atmosphere pretentiously reminiscent of the luxury resorts of the East, well-to-do vacationers easily accepted small discomforts while they visited Yellowstone's wonders.

The typical tour of Yellowstone began when the tourists, outfitted in petticoats, straw hats, and linen dusters (few were persuaded to buy dime-novel versions of western wear) descended from the train, boarded large stagecoaches, and headed up the scenic Gardner River canyon to Mammoth Hot Springs. After checking into a large hotel they were free the rest of the day to sit in a porch chair (perhaps the same one that President Arthur had used); to spend their money on such souvenirs as rocks, silver spoons, photos, and post card views of frontier characters like Calamity Jane; and to fraternize with Army officers and frontiersmen like Jack Baronett, who had built the first bridge over the Yellowstone. Most of the visitors spent the afternoon touring the hot springs terraces, under the guidance of a congenial soldier or hotel bellhop, or bathing in the water. Those who wanted to know more about the terraces, as Rudyard Kipling did in 1889, could purchase a guide to the formations "which some lurid hotel keeper has christened Cleopatra's Pitcher or Mark Anthony's Whiskey Jug, or something equally poetical." A heavy meal and retirement to a soft bed usually ended the tourist's first day in the park.

For the next 14 days, the tourists bounced along in four-horse, 11-passenger coaches called "Yellowstone wagons." They were entertained by the colorful profanity of the stage

"Barney at the back door." Living with wildlife is routine in Yellowstone, as this bear cub attached to the screen door of a Mammoth residence testifies.

Three prominent photographers, William H. Jackson, Frank Jay Haynes, and his son Jack Ellis Haynes, spanned nearly a hundred years of bringing images of Yellowstone to the public. Stereoscopes were a popular means of reliving a trip to Yellowstone.

drivers, who urged their horses over the dusty roads of the Grand Loop. During the several halts at important natural features, the drivers further amazed their passengers with exceedingly imaginary explanations of the natural history. At midday there was a pause for refreshment at a lunch stop like Larry's at Norris. Each night there was a warm bed and a lavish meal at another grand hotel, such as the elaborately rustic Old Faithful Inn or the more conventional but equally immense Lake Hotel.

Yellowstone did have a few genuine hazards for visitors. In 1877, as the Nez Perce Indians came through the park after the Battle of the Big Hole, they captured two tourist parties and killed or severely wounded a number of the people they encountered. The brief flurry of the Bannock War in 1878 raised fears of another Indian foray. These dangers were soon replaced by the occasional accidents of stagecoaching and the hazards that awaited the careless.

But the delights outweighed the perils. After the late 1890s people enjoyed the nightly spectacle of bears being fed hotel garbage and even helped with the feeding, few worrying about the effect on the bears or the danger to themselves. Some of the early tourists were even honored by the placement of their names on the map—in 1873 Mary Lake took the name of one of its first visitors, and in 1891 Craig Pass honored the first woman driven over it on a new road. And there was always the possibility that a tourist might rub elbows with a European nobleman or an American dignitary like President Theodore Roosevelt, who toured the park in 1903.

Some of the tourists availed themselves of optional pleasures. Boats offered peaceful tours of Yellowstone Lake, while back at Mammoth wildlife could be closely observed at the "game corral."

As a contrast to the elaborate hotels, rustic tent camps provided simple but comfortable accommodations among the trees. Uncle John Yancey's "Pleasant Valley Hotel" hosted teamsters and U.S. Senators alike. Uncle John, according to one patron, was a "goat-bearded, shrewd-eyed, lank, Uncle Sam type," whose unkempt hotel offered those of simpler taste welcome relief from the opulence of the great resorts in the park. And one guest noted that "A little bribe on the side and a promise to keep the act of criminality a secret from Uncle John induces the maid to provide us with clean sheets." The affability of Uncle John was later matched by the wholesome friendliness of Uncle Tom Richardson, who served splendid picnics at his trail into the canyon.

Altogether, touring Yellowstone was a pleasant, if arduous, experience. But the reactions of some visitors were not always what might be expected, according to a stage driver: "I drive blame curious kind of folk through this place. Blame curious. Seems a pity that they should a come so far just to liken Norris to hell. Guess Chicago would have served them, speakin' in comparison, just as good." In keeping with the unspoken rules of the wealthy tourist's social class—which required a calm demeanor at all times—few of the many photographs taken during Grand Tours show smiles on the dignified faces posed among the natural wonders. Yet the "dudes" carried home memories of experiences and sights that were unforgettable. They recommended the tour to their friends, and each year more of them came to Yellowstone to gaze upon its wonders.

But as increasing wealth and technological progress enabled more of the public to travel, Yellowstone could not remain an idyllic resort for the few. The first automobile entered Yellowstone in 1902, only to be evicted because regulations had already been adopted to exclude such conveyance. Yet "progress" could not be staved off forever. Over the years the pressure mounted. Political favor swung toward cars, and many people foresaw benefits in admitting them to the park. Accordingly, in 1915, the Secretary of the Interior made the fateful decision, and on July 31 of that year cars began to invade Yellowstone. Although they were severely regulated and a permit was expensive, their numbers increased steadily, forcing the concessioners to replace their stages with buses. Horses were relegated to the back country, while many of the tent camps, hotels, lunch stations, and eventually all but

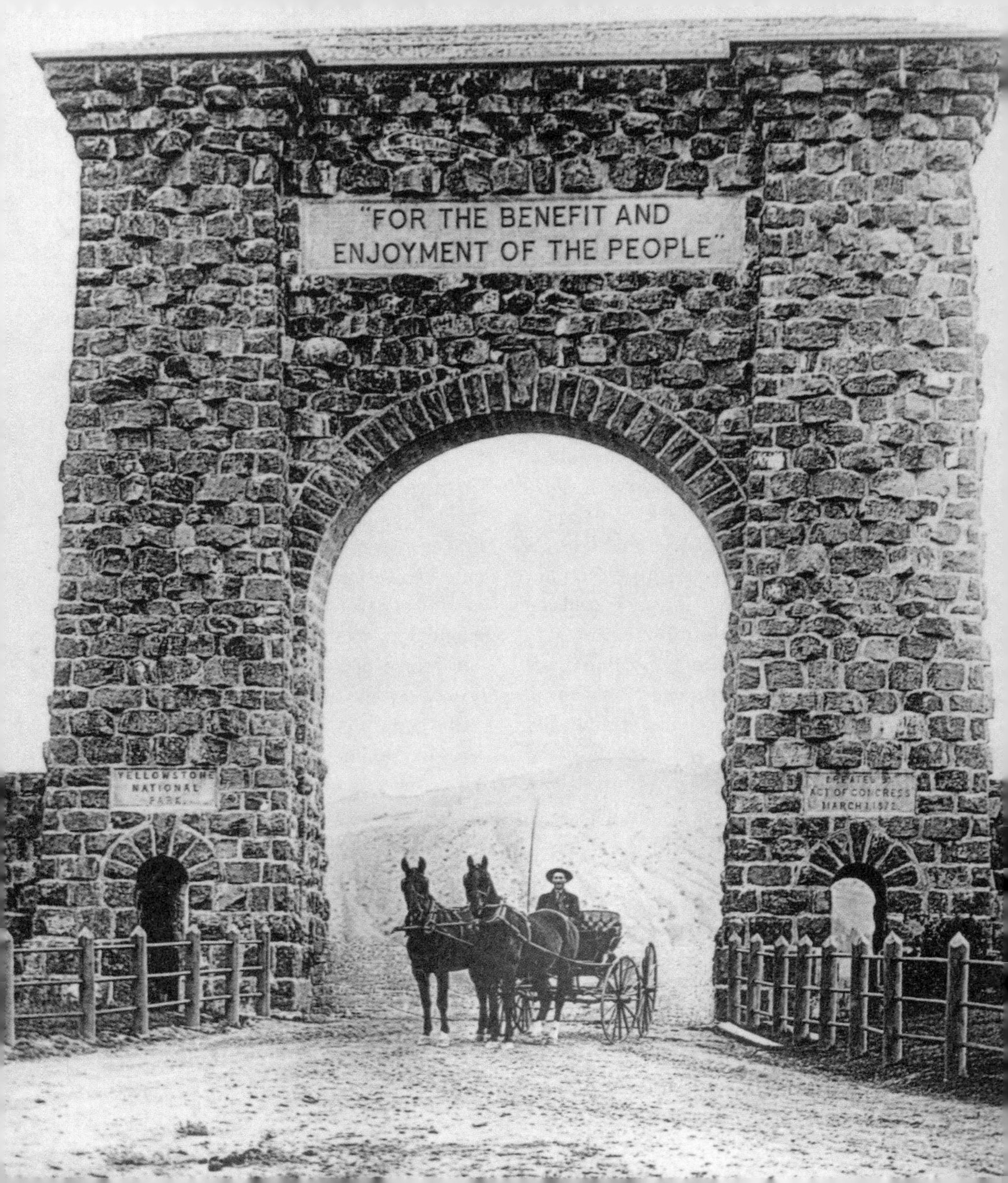
"FOR THE BENEFIT AND
ENJOYMENT OF THE PEOPLE"
YELLOWSTONE
NATIONAL

one of the transportation companies disappeared. They were replaced by paved roads, parking areas convenient to scenic attractions, service stations, and public campgrounds to accommodate the growing number of motorized visitors.

But the automobile changed more than just the mode of touring the park. No longer just a vacation spot for the wealthy, Yellowstone became a truly *national* park, accessible to anyone who could afford a car. Without resorting to the concessioners, visitors could now pick their own way around the park, see what they wanted, take side trips, and camp in one place as long as they liked. But never again would a visitor be a pioneer explorer, facing an unknown wilderness, leaving his name on the map. For better or worse, a new day was beginning. The time lay far in the future when the car would appear as an enemy threatening to suffocate the park; meanwhile, it was all to the good. Thanks to this noisy, smoking, democratic vehicle, Yellowstone was now truly a "pleasuring-ground" for the people—all of them.

THE LEGACY OF YELLOWSTONE

The generation that set aside Yellowstone National Park created more than anyone could have foreseen at the time. The establishment of the park was initially a negative reaction to the prospect that this wondrous region might be divided and exploited for private ends, thereby denying it to others. The founders determined that Yellowstone should be reserved for the "benefit and enjoyment" of all. Over a half century, the practicalities of what such a national park should be were worked out.

Yet Yellowstone was always more than a place for frolic in the wilderness. The park was something to be proud of, and its creators exhibited their pride throughout their lives. It was a pride that came not from "civilizing" the wilderness but from knowing that a place of wild beauty had been preserved. Yellowstone was, as they saw it, their gift to the people.

But their gift was greater than even they realized at the time. The years have shown that their legacy, the establishment of Yellowstone National Park, led to a lasting concept—the national park idea. This idea conceived the wilderness to be the inheritance of all the people, who gained more from an experience in nature than from private exploitation of the land. In time, the idea blossomed in the form of many new national parks, begotten in the same spirit as Yellowstone.

The national park idea was part of a new view of the Nation's responsibility for the public domain. By the end of the 19th century, many thoughtful people no longer believed that the wilderness should be fair game for the first persons who could claim and plunder it. Its fruits were the rightful possession of all the people, including those yet unborn. Besides the areas set aside as national parks, still greater expanses of land were placed into trusteeship in national forests and other reserves so that the country's wealth—in the form of lumber, grazing, minerals, and recreation—should not be consumed at once by the greed of a few, but should perpetually bestow its rewards.

The preservation idea, born in Yellowstone spread around the world. Scores of nations have preserved areas of natural beauty and historical worth so that all mankind will have the opportunity to reflect on their natural and cultural heritage, and to return to nature and be spiritually reborn in it.

Of all the benefits from Yellowstone National Park, this may be the greatest.

Other Yellowstone books by HOMESTEAD PUBLISHING

YELLOWSTONE: SELECTED PHOTOGRAPHS 1870-1960 with introduction by
Senator Alan Simpson, edited by Carl Schreier
THE GRAND TETONS: THE STORY OF TAMING THE WESTERN WILDERNESS by
Margaret Sanborn
A FIELD GUIDE TO YELLOWSTONE'S GEYSERS, HOT SPRINGS AND FUMAROLES by
Carl Schreier
YELLOWSTONE EXPLORERS GUIDE by Carl Schreier